# ROGUES, HOBOES, AND ENTREPRENEURS:

## COPING WITH THE GREAT DEPRESSION

Greetings, Mrs Beck,

I hope you have as much fun reading this book as I had writing it.

Truly,
Cy W Greenhalgh

# ROGUES, HOBOES, AND ENTREPRENEURS:

## COPING WITH THE GREAT DEPRESSION

By
CY W. GREENHALGH

Drawings by
ROBERT L. CARDIN

ISBN: 1-58820-086-8

1stBooks - rev. 10/06/00

## This book is dedicated

To my daughters Linda, Jo Ann, Judith, Susan, and Cindy, who as toddlers kept me busy telling them stories of my misspent youth. That retelling has kept fresh in my mind the episodes recounted in this book.

And to my wife Marge, who listened to my tales with tortured forbearance, and on social occasions rescued me from embarrassment when I remembered the smallest detail from the past but forgot how many times I had told it to the same person.

## Deep appreciation is expressed

To Bob Cardin for his line drawings, to Anne Schaetzel for getting me started writing this book, to Alice Speil and Jean wayne for their help, to members of the Sun City West Desert Writer's Guild for critiquing the manuscript, especially Thayer Soule for editorial guidance and many substantive suggestions, to my wife Marge and daughters Susan and Jo Ann for their help, and to all my daughters for their encouragement.

# CONTENTS

"Pappy," chief of the entrepreneurial clan, primed to lasso one of his six mischievous sons in this 1925 photograph

# PREFACE

What was life like for kids in a frontier mining town of the American West at the outset of the Great Depression? For youths living through it? For young entrepreneurs striving for something better? I address the subject as one of those kids/youths/entrepreneurs who was born in 1914 at Silver City, Utah, third in a family of six boys.

The rumble of a freight train stirs memories of that life and my days as a teen-age hobo riding the rails on a journey into the unknown. I was caught up in events too vast for me to comprehend. or for society to control. This book describes that journey and the period in which it occurred. The story is told in three parts.

Part 1 narrates the adventures and misadventures of boys who were reared in the Tintic Mining District of Utah. We were mischievous rogues given to impish tricks. Our wayward behavior sometimes got us in trouble.

Included are tales from the 1920s – tales of youthful fascination with cars, horses, and guns, with rabbit shoots and community celebrations, with projects to earn spending money, and with work. If we hit upon work we found ways to get some fun out of it. As our boypower developed into manpower the fun ran out. We found, as the depression deepened, that our manpower was not worth much.

Part 2 tells of hobo life during the depth of the Great Depression in the 1930s. It is about hopping freights while evading bulls, and riding the rails in search of work. Harvesting seasonal crops required manpower and sometimes horsepower. Hoboes provided the manpower and semi-wild mustangs provided the horsepower. When the job was done both were turned loose. The horses were fortunate. They found better sustenance in the nearby hills than the hoboes found in the outside world.

Food was our top preoccupation. When riding the rails from job to job we knew hunger – gnawing, day-after-day, deep down hunger. A Mulligan stew, prepared in the jungle where each hobo added to the pot and all shared the delight, satisfied hunger. It also provided camaraderie for the soul, without which many souls would have burst. Food meant more to us than wages. Sex was not important. Maybe that was because we didn't have the energy, maybe because there were few women around.

Life was rough, but along the way we found inspiration from others who shared what little they had.

Part 3 is about those who thought it better to try something even if they failed, than to try nothing and succeed in nothing. The Great Depression stimulated the entrepreneurial spirit. Many frustrated persons tried to do something, anything. Otherwise their lives would fall apart, as had the world around them.

The New Deal Administration tried to do something – many things – to stimulate the economy. Most of the things it did provided only temporary relief. One action, however, had a permanent effect on the country as a whole, and on my family in particular. That was to devalue the dollar. To take advantage of the increased prices of gold and silver, we set out to strike it rich, mining in the Tintic Hills.

The first chapter provides background on the Tintic Mining District in Utah, where much of the action takes place. The glossary at the end of the text clarifies the meaning of terms seldom used today but common in the vernacular of transients and laborers in the 1930s.

The Japanese attack at Pearl Harbor on December 7, 1941 signalled the end of the Great Depression. It also broke up the family mining enterprise, and shattered the entrepreneurial spirit upon which it was based.

**Rogues, hoboes, entrepreneurs in their Sunday best.**
**Dick, Marlin, Dave, Cy, Wayne, Jack, and Parents**

# PART 1

# ROGUES

# Chapter 1

# Short History of the Tintic Mining District

The discovery of rich mineral deposits near Silver City, Utah, was made by a party of Mormons, in defiance of the strictures of their church. In its boisterous heyday Silver City suffered the pains of ethnic and religious rivalries. These pains grew out of the unusual manner in which Utah Territory was settled by the Mormons.

Soon after Brigham Young led his brigade of Latter-Day-Saints into the Salt Lake Valley in 1847, he sent out small parties of brethren to establish farming communities. He exhorted his flock never to condone the rip-roaring kinds of towns that come with mining. "Touch it not. Cleave to the soil. Your eyes see gold and silver. I see a yoke of bondage."

In 1862 General Patrick E. Connor was ordered to Utah, ostensibly to guard the mails and the immigrant trails, but actually to keep a weather eye on Brigham Young and his followers. Brigham's view of miners as the riffraff and scum of humanity was seen in a different light by General Pat, a staunch Irish Catholic. Many of his volunteers were Gentiles (in Mormon terms, non-believers) drawn from the California mining districts. The wily old General granted them furloughs for prospecting trips into the surrounding hills. He knew, as did Brigham, that mining drew Gentiles, and Gentiles would challenge the monopoly of the Mormon Church.

With the arrival of General Connor's troops, depredations by the Utes Tribe were brought under control, and a few isolated ranches were developed in the flatlands to the west of the Tintic Hills. Reports that a cowboy from one of the ranches had found a piece of high-grade float (an isolated chunk of ore) generated

3

great interest, even among the Mormon faithful. That float, they reasoned, had been carried by the rains from a higher elevation, from an outcrop of ore in the nearby hills.

These reports gained glitter in the telling. Six young Mormon farmers, ignoring the cautions of their elders, formed a prospecting party to find the source of that float. After several days of fruitless search they camped at a spring near the site of the future town, Silver City. During the night a brisk wind blew a dusting of snow from a nearby ledge. When the leaders of the party investigated the barren ledge they found, beyond their wildest dreams, an outcropping of virgin ore. They named their claim the Sunbeam, after the sun that beamed through the foreboding clouds. The date was December 13, 1869.

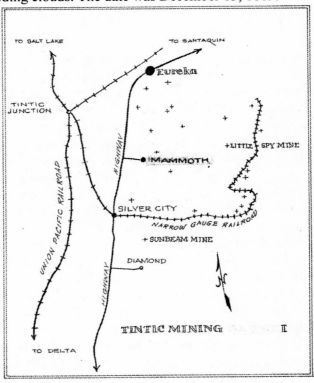

**Map of the Tintic Mining District.**

The Sunbeam lode was only the first of many discoveries in the Tintic hills. News of the strike spread rapidly. The influx of prospectors and miners grew from a trickle to a torrent. The Tintic Mining District was established, and four towns were laid out: Diamond, after the sparkling quartz crystals found; Silver City, after the horn silver of the Sunbeam lode; Mammoth, after the size of the ore deposits envisioned; and Eureka, after the triumphant phrase "I've found it!"

As the mining district matured, Diamond was abandoned. Only the graveyard, with markers decayed by the raw elements, remained. Eureka and Mammoth boomed with riches, but suffered the turmoil that riches brought. Silver City developed as a town of about a thousand souls, a stable town by mining camp standards. It was a tribute to the residents, reared amidst rivalries, that a tranquil atmosphere existed. The harmonious feel of the town induced my parents to settle and raise their family in that "rootin-tootin" but friendly mining camp.

In 1909 my father finished a job as millwright in the construction of an ice-making plant. Before turning to new ventures he returned to the farming community of his birth, Santaquin, Utah, and decided to continue his schooling. He found the "school marm" more interesting than the school, and proposed marriage. The school marm, a Gentile, talked to David's mother, a Mormon, to see if a conflict might develop. "Jessie," the mother said, "David is an impossible scamp. From the day he could walk he's given me more heartache than all of his six brothers put together. But he has also given me more pleasure. If you can handle him, you've got my blessing."

Jessie was madly in love with this irrepressible optimist who had returned, at age 27, to obtain his grammar school diploma. She accepted David's proposal and they were married in 1910. They settled in Silver City and had six sons, typical mining camp rogues, full of mischief, every one.

A special year for me was 1914, the year I was born. It was not so special for my mother, who had already borne two sons and yearned for a daughter. My birth as a boy disappointed her. So did the birth of three other boys who followed. After six fruitless yearnings, she abandoned hope for a daughter and devoted her energies to civilizing her six rambunctious sons. That was a tough assignment in a place where mere survival was the measure of success.

For residents of Silver City, the "great crash of twenty-nine" was merely another blast in a continuing storm. In the 1920's they saw their town deteriorate from boom to bust. In 1931 they abandoned it, a ghost town marked only by a sign at the side of the road: <u>Silver City</u>.

# Chapter 2

# Escapades of Untamed Rogues

Boys reared in a frontier mining camp were untamed rogues. We were untamed not for lack of parental guidance or as unprincipled scoundrels; we were just mischievous scamps looking for ways to expend our youthful energy. I was fortunate. Without getting into too much mischief, I found ways to satisfy my passion for automobiles, my love of horses, and my fascination with guns.

In the summer of 1929, just before my fifteenth birthday, Carl Galloway offered me a job pumping gas at his filling station in Eureka. A job at twenty-five cents an hour was too good to pass up. I took it, even though his station was five miles from my home in Silver City. Getting back and forth posed a problem, but I handled that by hitch-hiking to work and snitching a ride home on Denver & Rio Grande Western freight trains

After getting a feel for the job I made myself useful pumping gas, fixing flat tires, changing oil, and keeping the station tidy. With growing self-confidence, I approached Carl on a subject that had been gnawing at me for some time. "Carl," I said, "what's the story on that Hupmobile touring car in the back yard? It looks to me like it's been abandoned."

"It has been abandoned, you might say. I took it in on a bad debt last spring and the guy never came back to claim it. If you want it, you can have it for the twenty-five dollars he owes me. The trouble is, I don't have the registration papers so you can't get it licensed."

On that basis I bought this 1922 Hupmobile touring car. I could hardly wait to get her on the road. It proved to be a dandy car except for two things: The tires were bald, and it used a gallon of oil for every tank of gas. To solve the tire problem I cut the steel rims off   a set of discarded oversize tires, and forced one of the carcasses over each of the bald ones on the car. This provided double protection, but it made the speedometer register too low. Sometimes that worked to my advantage. If I had a timid passenger out for a spin and she complained about going too fast I could say, "No, the speedometer shows we're doing only fifty," when to my secret satisfaction I knew that we were speeding right along.

**This 1922 Hupmobile for twenty five dollars? It's a deal!**

The oil problem was not serious. The car didn't burn oil; it just had a leak around the pan gasket. I figured that until I could replace the gasket, I'd salvage the best of the crankcase oil drained from other cars, strain it, and carry it with me for use as required.

I wasn't concerned about driving without license plates. Cops in the district were casual about minor infractions of the law. They didn't take action unless pressured to do so, and who would complain about a kid driving an unlicensed automobile?

When school started, my work at the filling station was limited to weekends because on school days we had football practice. The school bus couldn't wait for the three kids from Silver City who were on the team, so my Hupmobile came in handy to get us home.

One day the principal approached me. "Cy," he said, "the coach told me that you haul the out-of-town football players home after practice. That's nice of you and handy for us, but it makes your car a quasi-official school bus and it ought to be legal. Here is ten dollars to pay for a license, and I'll arrange with Randall's service station to give you a gallon of gas for each school day. Okay?"

Being unaccustomed to receiving windfalls of this magnitude, I accepted the contribution gratefully. However, I wondered how I could manage to fulfill my part of the bargain. Without registration papers, I couldn't get a license.

That afternoon I found that sometimes good luck does indeed strike twice. On my way home from school, as was my habit, I stopped at the Tintic Bakery. The bakery made cream puffs that were delicious when fresh, but sour when held without refrigeration to the next day. The truck driver delivered these delicacies to stores in the morning and late in the afternoon retrieved the ones not sold. Those were thrown out with the garbage. Being allergic to waste, I endeavored to salvage, by personal consumption, as many of those cream puffs as a healthy young man's constitution could absorb.

The winsome young lady behind the counter was a gracious collaborator. I told her of my good fortune and the problem I faced in getting a set of license plates. I must have been talking in a voice louder than I normally used when in her company. Dave Hunter, the baker, approached me from the rear of the shop.

"Cy," he said, "I've got the solution to your problem. I just bought a new car at Conover's Garage and they wouldn't give me a damn cent as a trade-in on my Model-T bug. So I've got it and no place to put it. I'll tell you what I'll do. I'll sell you the license plates for ten bucks and throw in the Ford, all registered, to boot."

Needless to say, I accepted his generous offer. From that time forward I had a set of wheels under me – legal wheels, almost. For school days I transferred the license plates to my Hupmobile and hauled the gang around town. For weekends I transferred the plates back to my Model-T bug and chauffeured my girl friend around the countryside.

* * * *

Being the owner of two automobiles at age fifteen, I was a proud young man. I was doubly proud when I became half-owner of a motorcycle. Some buddies who had been scrounging the Eureka dump told about a motorcycle that had been discarded. I related this momentous information to my brother Marlin and we checked it out. It was a Harley Davidson-74 from which the motor and various accessories had been removed. It wasn't much of a motorcycle, but it was a frame with handlebars and tires.

"Let's push her home and fix her up," Marlin said, "I know where we can get an Indian-61 motor, and we'll figure out how to make her run."

We pushed our motorcycle home and showed it to "Pappy." Our father didn't like formality. We called him Pappy. He remarked, "Hmmm, I see where my shop is going to be a busy place this summer."

Marlin was a natural mechanic who devoted his free time to figuring out what made things work, and if they didn't, how to make them work. Pappy's shop was Marlin's laboratory, where he built miniature steam engines, repaired carburetors, and investigated the marvels of whatever struck his fancy. He sometimes left his projects in scattered disarray.

Although our stripped-down motorcycle was heavy, I had great fun pushing it up the hill in front of our house and coasting back down. It was the nearest thing to a bicycle that we had ever possessed. Only rich city kids had bicycles.

When Marlin completed his bargaining and returned with the Indian-61 motor we went to work in earnest. We took the motor apart and laid out the pieces for inspection and repair. As I cleaned them Marlin examined, adjusted, honed as necessary, and put them back together. We started her up. On idle she purred like a pussy cat. On full throttle she roared like a lion.

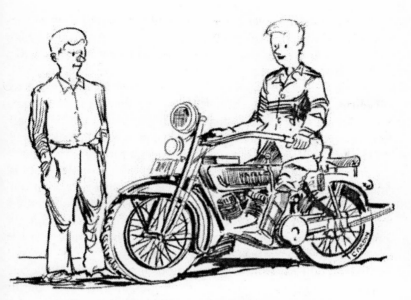

**Proud mechanics admire their motorcycle.**

The Indian-61 was a smaller motorcycle than the Harley-74. To mount a small motor in a large frame required ingenuity. Marlin figured out what to do, and I helped him do it. "Cy," he said, "make a fire in the forge. Start with soft coal, then add anthracite, and finally some coke. When the fire's going real hot, bank it and ease up on the blower."

"I've cranked the blower plenty of times for Pappy," I responded, "so I'll handle the forge and keep the iron hot." My testiness withered as the smoke of the fire blossomed into the white heat of a mature forge fire. How different it is, I mused, to work for yourself. Turning the crank on the blower becomes not a chore but a pleasant, rhythmic challenge. Smelling the acrid smoke becomes not an annoyance but a symbol of accomplishment. Feeling the heat of the fire becomes not a discomfort but a measure of success. Watching Marlin pound and shape the brackets and filler pieces from the irons heated red in the forge becomes not wasted time but pure delight.

News of our project soon circulated among the kids of the town, and thence to their parents. Interest was keen, and we had lots of help collecting the parts we needed to get our rig on the road. Many of the men about town had motorcycles in their youth and had stashed away mementos which they donated to the cause. We collected and installed a kickstand, a tandem seat, a speedometer with a cable that fit, headlights and tail lights, all that we needed to complete the job. The man who had discarded his Harley-74 gave us the registration papers for it.

Everyone in town enjoyed the sight of a couple of kids riding their new toy with abandon. Everyone, that is, except our mother. Although proud of our performance, she was concerned for our safety. In raising us she never said no to our requests unless there was a compelling reason to do so. Her concern for our safety in this case was not that compelling.

Marlin and I both relished riding our motorcycle. However, he preferred to have four wheels under him, and manoeuvered to get them. One time we visited our Uncle Henry, a farmer who lived in Santaquin. After we helped him put up hay for several days, Marlin broached the subject of his interest. "Uncle Henry," he said, "what are you going to do with that old Ford out back of the chicken coop?"

"Well, I'll tell you," Henry replied. "I'm not going to do anything with it. In 1917, when I bought it brand-new in Payson, the salesman knew enough to fill it with gas but he didn't know that it needed water in the radiator, and neither did I. Cars were just coming on the market in them days. Half way home the engine got hot and froze up on me. I didn't know what to do, so I just dragged it home with a team of horses. I put it on wood blocks back of the chicken coop and covered it up with a tarpaulin. I'd like to get it out of the yard. If you want it, you can have it."

Marlin jumped at the offer. He pumped up the tires, removed the blocks, and went to work on the motor. He removed the head from the engine and found that with a little oil on the cylinder walls the pistons could be cranked around freely. He put gas in the tank, tinkered with the carburetor and the coils,

12

turned the crank a few times with appropriate choking, and it sputtered. He tinkered some more and cranked some more, and a second cylinder started to fire, then the third and fourth. She had started right up.

Marlin now had four wheels under him, a 1917 Model-T Ford that had been driven a mere three miles. It was a good Ford, but it was heavy and didn't have much speed going uphill. We removed the body and she drove like a jackrabbit, but then there was no gas tank. The tank was part of the body, not the chassis. Until Marlin could figure a way to attach a gas tank to his stripped-down Ford, he commandeered me or one of the younger brothers to ride with him. When the engine gasped for gasoline we poured some directly into the gas line from a squirt can that we carried at the ready. We refilled the squirt can from a one-gallon coal oil can.

Ford Model-Ts of that vintage had a steering mechanism which sometimes sent the car awry. Marlin discovered that peculiarity when he was showing off at the high school, driving slalom fashion among the parked cars and buildings. The steering mechanism, instead of turning the car as expected, locked firm in the extreme, rammed into a building, and threw him over the hood. He survived that incident with tolerable grace but wounded pride.

"Let's drive her home, Cy," he said, "and see how we can fix her." He took the steering mechanism apart, studied it piece by piece, and finally offered judgment: "This problem can't be fixed, Cy. It's a quirk of early Model-Ts. A fellow just has to learn how to drive the old baby."

Marlin's Ford, our jointly owned motorcycle, my Hupmobile, and my Ford were the envy of all the kids in town. My passion for automobiles was satisfied.

\* \* \* \*

Ranking only slightly below my passion for automobiles was my love of horses. I was able to gratify that love when Roy Lazzenbee arrived in Silver City and assumed squatter's rights to the Stark homestead on the western fringe of town.

Bill Stark had filed on 160 acres of flat prairie under the Homestead Act. He cleared the land of sagebrush, rocks, and trees, then fenced it with posts cut from the junipers. He planted Turkey Red wheat, the variety favored by dry-farmers who depended upon rain to water their crops. Year after year the rains didn't come at the proper season, so there was scant harvest. Most of the sparse grain that did grow was devoured by jackrabbits.

Bill Stark was an able farmer, but after a spell of lean years about the only food he could provide his family was boiled wheat and alfalfa porridge. "Alfalfa," he joked, "makes healthy kids." His survival farm didn't provide survival, so he packed up his family and moved away.

When Roy Lazzenbee moved into the abandoned Stark homestead, things began to happen. To my delight, he had horses.

Roy was readily recognized as a newcomer to this mining camp. He was slight of build and wiry, not muscular from hard labor but lithe and quick of movement. He wore a denim jacket and Levis tucked into cowboy boots. Those boots were well-worn working boots, plain without fancy stitching. Under the brow of his wide-brim hat gazed squinting eyes. Where they blended into his leathery face permanent wrinkles had formed. This man had faced the heat of summer sun and the cold of winter air. His life was not that of an underground miner.

Roy made a thorough study of the homestead. "This spread is no good as a dry farm," he told his wife. "I'll build some corrals and do what I know best, work with animals." He had worked with sheep, cattle, and horses. His specialty was horses, wild ones. As a mustanger from Nevada, he knew the habits of wild horses and how to capture them. As a bronco-buster, he knew how to break them, to saddle and subdue them. As a shrewd operator, he knew how to make money from them.

Roy had some good riding horses. With the help of his two sons he began rounding up wild horses on the open range. Wild horses, variously called broncos, mustangs, or rangs, were small. Although agile, fast, and great fun to ride when properly broken,

14

they couldn't match the speed of Roy's horses on the open range.

Roy made a business of breaking his mustangs to saddle, and renting them out as riding ponies at twenty-five cents an hour. From the outset I was his best customer, riding his most skittish broncos. In short order he made me an offer: "Cy, help me on the roundup and you can ride my mustangs for free."

"It's a deal!"

"Let's start in the morning, about five o'clock," Roy said. "Bring a canteen of water and a hearty lunch. We might be late getting back." About daybreak Roy, his two sons and I, left for what he called the watering hole, some fifteen miles to the southwest. As we rode off, Roy filled me in on the habits of wild horses and outlined his plans.

"Wild hosses take on water every coupla days. That's why I want to start at the watering hole. These mustangs seem awful fast, but that's 'cause they're small, maybe six to eight hundred pounds. They're no match for my hosses at ten hundred or so. But the rangs don't carry a man and a saddle, and they have stamina. So we want to approach 'em from the far side of the ranch. That way, when we spook 'em, they run in the right direction.

"The average band has maybe half a dozen mares, a few colts, and one stallion. He's the leader and the protector of his harem. He's spookier'n hell. The colts hang around till they're about three years old. From then on the fillies, the young mares, stay with the harem, and the frisky young studs get kicked out by the stallion. He don't want no competition.

"Young studs, they run together and develop their strength and fighting ability. When they're about six years old they get cocky and their leader challenges an old stallion for his harem. If he gets the best of the fight, the old boy slinks off in despair. We sometimes see these old battlers all alone on the range."

We traveled far and wide. As we rode over one ridge we came face to face with a band of antelope. They stared at us briefly, then fled single file at remarkable speed. Roy said, "Them critters have got more curiosity than fear. It's a good thing they've got keen eyes and fast feet or there wouldn't be no more antelope."

Late in the day we spotted a band of mustangs streaking west. Roy said, "I reckon we can't get around to the far side and bring 'em in before nightfall. We might as well mosey back to the ranch."

The next day we had better luck. With binoculars we could see one band drinking at the watering hole, and another browsing while waiting its turn. Roy said, "Now there's a typical display of animal etiquette if ever I seen one. Let's wait for that old stallion and his harem to leave. Then we'll round up the second band. It's a shame to pick on the polite ones, but I can count nine young studs, and that's what we want."

At Roy's signal we approached that band. His two sons raced forward, one to each side. I followed at the rear, and Roy served as point guard wherever needed. The young studs were frantic with fear, but unable to outrun our horses. We corralled them without incident. Roy pleased me by observing, "A fourth man on the crew sure does make the job run smooth."

Corralling a band of rangs was only the first step in Roy's venture, as he explained to me: "Now I've got to figure out what to do with 'em. Wild hosses are spirited critters. Some of 'em will resist capture with their last breath. Some will refuse to eat or drink. Some just give up and die. Some will live, but are so broken in spirit they'll never be no good. We'll just leave 'em to settle down for a few days. If some turn up losers I'll sell 'em to the State fish hatchery at fifteen dollars a head. The rest I'll break to ride. There again some of 'em might show up no good except for fish feed.

"I might end up with five or six nice young stud-hosses. I'll rent 'em out as riding ponies at two-bits an hour when they're half broke and four-bits when full broke. Sheepherders and farmers pay thirty five dollars a head for a good pony. Cy, I'm happy to have you along to help round 'em up. I hope you're happy to ride the half broke ones for free."

We both were happy with that.

\* \* \* \*

16

Outranked only by my passion for automobiles and my love of horses was my fascination with guns. This derived from my childhood anticipation of community rabbit hunts. Jackrabbits were the scourge of sagebrush country. Rabbit hunts were frequently staged to kill off some of them. Hunts sometimes began with a baseball game between the married men and the single men of Silver City. Admission was free. However, generous spectators purchased "I'm No Piker" tickets for a dollar. They displayed them prominently in their hatbands to show their generosity and support.

After the baseball game, the sportsmen of town lined up abreast about fifteen yards apart. As they sallied forth with shotguns at the ready, the married bucks and the single bucks were positioned alternately. Each participant was allowed to shoot only the rabbits that jumped up within his designated swath.

As the hunters moved forward they sliced off the tails of their kill for use in determining the winning team. The tails from each side were tallied. Members of the winning team were honored guests at a community feed. Men from the losing team paid for it.

This community gathering was a big affair. While the hunters were attacking their prey, the women were preparing a feed of baked beans, hot dogs, potato salad, and all the fixings. At the conclusion of the celebration a grand prize was awarded to the man who had collected the greatest number of jackrabbit tails. Each hunter was allowed only two boxes of shotshells. Fifty tails normally represented a perfect score. My father occasionally exceeded that score by shooting two rabbits with one shot. He was frequently the exalted winner. I sought to emulate his example. Thus my interest in guns.

I won my first shotgun in the second Dempsey-Tunney fight. It was held in Chicago on my 13th birthday, September 22, 1927. I took a gambling chance and bet three dollars against a sawed-off double barrel shotgun. Tunney won the fight on a ten-round decision. I won the bet. That was a good thing because I didn't know where I could scare up three dollars if I lost.

To celebrate my good fortune, two buddies joined me on a jackrabbit hunt. Dobie Winch was carrying my sawed-off shotgun, foolishly swinging it cocked with his finger on the trigger. When he crawled across a barbed wire fence it went off, and the charge hit Mac Bigler in the foot.

Following that escapade we took plenty of flack from our parents. We promised to do better next time. "There won't be no next time," Mac's father said.

Mac was the fastest-running halfback on our football team and the best-scoring forward on our basketball team. The coach gave us a blistering that lasted all season. The doctor plucked shot pellets from Mac's foot throughout the entire autumn. We suffered a poor sports record that year.

Pappy destroyed my shotgun.

\*　\*　\*　\*

I had what kids called a blunderbuss, a .22 caliber pistol converted from a rifle. I had sawed off the barrel of a single-shot rifle, removed the stock, and bent the tang to accept a pistol grip fashioned after the Colt Frontier revolver. It was a dandy weapon but it had one defect. The hammer was improperly aligned with the rim of the cartridge. Sometimes several tries were required to make it fire.

One evening some of us were playing cops and robbers. One of the cops, after several misfires of my blunderbuss, pointed it over the head of my brother Dick, who was one of the robbers. Dick raised his hands in surrender just as the cop pulled the trigger again. This time it fired. The bullet hit Dick in the palm and lodged part way up his arm. The other cops and robbers disappeared. Dick and I scurried to find Pappy.

"It's a damn shame the bullet didn't go all the way through," he said. "The doctor might have to do a lot of probing to find it. Get hold of your mother, Cy, and we'll high-tail for the Payson hospital."

Dick was stoic throughout the ordeal until the doctor tied his arms to the operating table. Having accepted Mother's assurance that the operation would be a simple matter, he was not prepared to be strapped helpless. Why was this necessary? What was coming next? Was it that dreaded chloroform? Yes, it was chloroform. Dick resisted by holding his breath. As the anaesthetic took effect he choked and writhed in convulsions. "Doctor," the nurse cried, "he's turning blue!"

"My God," the doctor said, "he's swallowed his tongue!"

The doctor retrieved Dick's tongue and continued the operation. The patient recovered.

Pappy destroyed my blunderbuss.

\* \* \* \*

My father had some surplus tools in his shop that Roy Lazzenbee wanted for use around his ranch. Roy, knowing my keen interest in guns, hatched a scheme. "Cy," he said, "if you can pry them tools loose from your dad, I'll trade you my .25:20 Winchester carbine for 'em."

I went to work on the idea. After sleeping on it, I said, "Pappy, I think I'll clean up your shop so we can find things when we want 'em. You might even want to discard some of the stuff you don't use any more."

That was all right with him. I did a good job of swamping out, placing things where they should be, and segregating surplus tools in one corner of the shop.

When Pappy got around to it, he looked things over. Only when he appeared suitably impressed did I outline the proposition that Roy had made to me, and display the tools he wanted. "Aha," Pappy said, "so that's what you had up your sleeve. I wondered what caused your sudden spurt of ambition."

I sheepishly confessed, but argued my case. "It's still a good bargain. You're only giving up some tools you don't use any more. Roy needs 'em, and I could use his gun. Besides, we're making some room in the shop. Everybody wins."

"It's a good bargain for you, with nothing to lose and everything to gain. All right, Cy, you schemed this one out pretty good. I guess you deserve to win."

I was surprised that my father sanctioned this trade. Although he had destroyed my shotgun and my blunderbuss, he was redeemed in my eyes by allowing the trade of his tools for my prized .25:20 Winchester carbine. This was not a boy's plaything. It was a man's gun, a rifle suitable for hunting coyotes, bobcats, and other varmints.

I had arrived.

# Chapter 3

# Military Service for a Dollar a Day

Having arrived at the pinnacle of a boy's life, I faced a changed world in the fall of 1928 when my family moved to Provo so my brother Dave could start college.

Friendless in a strange town, with no horses to ride and no money to spend, I enrolled as a freshman at the local high school. I learned that the 145th Field Artillery, Utah National Guard, was seeking recruits for a cavalry unit stationed across town, and the pay was a dollar for every training session attended. "Aha, cavalry means horses, and the money looks good," I reasoned. "Maybe they won't take me at fourteen into a man's army, but I'll give it a whirl. As the gamblers say, nothing ventured, nothing gained."

At the armory the sergeant looked me over closely. "We've got two application forms here," he said. "If you're over eighteen but not twenty-one, you need a parent's consent. If you're twenty-one, there are no questions asked." He raised a skeptical eyebrow. My spirits withered. After a moment of agonizing suspense he continued, "Which one do you want?" My spirits rebounded.

I knew that my mother wouldn't lie for me, so I said, "I'll go for twenty-one." True to his statement, there were no questions asked. I signed the enlistment form. He stamped approval. I suddenly skipped seven years.

Every Monday night I learned about artillery, field manoeuvers, and the military way of handling horses. And I earned a dollar. It was a fun time, but as summer approached I gave my captain the sad news. "When school's out we're moving back to Silver City, so I'll have to muster out."

"Don't be in a hurry," he said. "Take a leave and come back for our ten-day field encampment at Camp Williams. It'll make a man out of you." And it means ten easy dollars, I thought. Agreed.

Camp Williams was in a desolate area between Salt Lake City and Provo known as Jordan Narrows. It had a firing range, tents for the men, corrals for the horses, sheds for the artillery pieces, and a barren parade ground of hard-packed clay.

When I arrived at the encampment late in the day I learned the meaning of military protocol and military discipline. "Inspection on the parade ground in fifteen minutes, private," growled the sergeant. "Your tent is the last one on line C. There's a tick on the cot. You won't have time to fill it with straw tonight. You can fill it in your free time, if you have any. Otherwise sleep on the bedspring. Serves ya damn well right."

At inspection I was found with wrinkled clothes, unruly hair, unpolished boots, and sullen demeanor -- dismally unfit as a soldier. In short, I was a private destined for special treatment called details.

Reveille was at 5:30 a.m., exercises at 6:00, breakfast at 7:00, artillery training until mid-afternoon, then liberty. At that point my special treatment began. Detail this, detail that: clean latrines, curry horses, pitch manure, double KP duty. Whatever detail came up, it was mine, the dirtier the better it seemed to me. Straw for my tick? No way!

The artillery pieces were "75s" as used by the French and American armies during the Great War. At the armory we had trained with dummy loads. At the firing line this was serious business with live loads almost three inches in diameter. The sergeant barked orders to his crew: "Load..Close Breach..Lock Break..Fire..Eject."

Competition for rapid-fire honors was keen. The battery from Salt Lake Company-A, eager to win, broke rhythm. What happened should not happen, could not happen, yet did happen. The gun fired before the breach was locked. The backfire explosion ripped across two men.

Pandemonium followed. All troops shared in the cleanup. My detail was quick to come: "Private, scour the parade ground for bits and pieces of flesh and bone. Cover the bits with dirt and gather the pieces in buckets for later disposal."

As the end of our field encampment drew near, I thought surely my good behavior entitled me to stand in the colonel's inspection on the last day. But no, I was given another detail: "Go down to the corral and groom the horses."

My buddy took me aside. "You're lucky, my friend, to be with the horses and not the troops. It doesn't bother the colonel to keep us standing hour after hour in the hot sun. As head honcho, he can just fold his arms at officers' attention and rest them on his big fat belly. The rest of us sweat it out at rigid attention. We can't even swat off the mosquitoes."

At the corral there were two gates, a narrow one normally left open for men to pass through, and a wide one normally kept closed for horses to pass through. As the inspection started, I entered the corral through the narrow gate. Immediately I was attracted to a big handsome black gelding. Captain Fuller had told me that he was the fastest horse in the camp, but an uncontrollable runaway. "Don't fuss with that old boy," he warned.

I looked that horse over, and he looked me over. I decided here's my chance to see who's boss. So I saddled and bridled him, and climbed aboard. We circled the corral a couple of times and I was feeling pretty cocky. Suddenly he pulled his head back, clenched the bit between his teeth, extended his head forward, and ran for the narrow gate. "Oh, baby," I said to myself, "I'm in deep trouble." I yanked the bridle so hard to the right that his head was crossways to his body, but still he raced toward the narrow gate. At the last moment, realizing that I could get my legs scraped off on the gate posts, I crossed them over the saddle horn, released tension on the bridle, and gave him his head.

The parade ground was on the beeline of his path. With nose stretched forward and ears laid back, he raced straight down the middle of the colonel's regimental inspection. Troops, in silent disbelief, lined one side of our path; officers, in apparent shock, lined the other. As we sped down the parade ground, I thought to myself, "What the hell, let her rip!" and leaned forward like a jockey in a tight race.

For a couple of miles that big beauty ran his heart out. Powerful beast though he was, however, he gradually tired. As he slowed, I realized I could get the best of him yet. "Okay, you Son-of-a-B," I said to him, "now it's my turn." I pulled him around and headed for the corral. He slowed down. I removed my belt and whipped him, right and left. The more he slowed, the more I whipped him. As we returned through the parade ground he was drenched with white lather. With head down and runaway spirit broken, he was subdued to a hangdog trot. The troops, ignoring protocol, gave me a roaring burst of applause.

Later, upon breaking camp, Captain Fuller broke protocol too, and addressed me by name rather than rank: "Good luck to you, Cy, you've earned your good-conduct discharge."

Maintaining discipline to the end, I said, "Thank you, sir."

To myself I thought, "and I've really earned my ten dollars."

**The runaway horse thinks he's the boss**

**The buckaroo shows who is the boss**

# Chapter 4

## Open Mouth Surgery

Doctors who practiced in frontier mining camps seldom had occasion to use psychology. Their patients were usually victims of accidents, or sufferers of chronic ailments. When the need arose, however, these country practitioners used medical expertise to cure physical ills, and subtle psychology to relieve mental anguish. Both skills were brought into play in keeping the kids of the camp healthy.

One day in the summer of 1929, Mother broke into the after-dinner banter among her six sons. "Boys, Doctor Osler will be making house calls in Silver City next Tuesday. If tonsillectomies are necessary, Doctor Bailey will serve as anaesthetist. Cy had no problem after his operation. I think we should have the rest of you taken care of too. Why don't you hold a powwow? If you can't think up any good objections, I'll call Doctor Osler and arrange it."

After a spirited council of war among us, Dave served as spokesman. "This is not really an objection, just a request. We have a ball game between upper-town and lower-town on Saturday. The earlier in the week the doctors can take us, the better we'll be healed by game time. We're short handed now, and if Marlin and I can't play, we'll have to forfeit the game for sure."

With no further requests and no comments audible to the parents, Mother made the arrangement. When she told Doctor Osler of the one request, he felt it was a reasonable proposition and scheduled his visit at our house for eight o'clock on the following Tuesday. "Prompt," he said.

The brothers had no concern about their operations. Throughout life their cuts and bruises had been stitched and salved by these doctors. Mother had no concern. She knew that

27

this team of country practitioners provided the ideal combination: professional care with a heart.

These doctors were as one in dedication, but vastly different in personality. Doctor Osler had large brown eyes that showed deep concentration when he was in thought, and a touch of humor when he was at ease. They were penetrating eyes that seemed to see beyond the vision of ordinary mortals. He used those eyes, his strong but nimble hands and sensitive fingers, his professionally trained intellect and skillfully honed senses, to perform miracles of medicine. He didn't aspire to higher station or an affluent practice. He didn't have, nor was he inclined to cultivate, a gracious bedside manner. He had a function to perform, and he performed it well.

Doctor Bailey was an impressive figure. Tall, slender, suave, and courtly, he was the epitome of a cultured southern gentleman. It was said that he could charm a dewdrop out of a cloud and lay it gently on the petal of a rose.

Because of failing eyesight, Doctor Bailey left his native Virginia to assume the less demanding assignment as "company doctor" at the hospital supported by the Mammoth Mine. In apparent compensation for his failing vision, he developed acute senses of sound, touch, and smell. He couldn't see well, but with guidance and support he could administer anaesthetic and monitor patients. As monitor, he could discern the slightest palpitation of a pulse, the slightest tremor of a voice. With his sensitive soul and delicate touch he could allay the anguish of a concerned mother, or the anxiety of a fearful child.

Precisely at eight o'clock on the scheduled morning the doctors arrived in the black Buick sedan that had carried Doctor Osler on many a mission for many a year. These doctors, Osler of the incisive mind and Bailey of the sensitive soul, entered the house, deposited their black bags on the sofa, and looked over the facilities.

Doctor Osler planned the procedure: "The dining room will be the operating room. The table, covered first with a blanket, then with a sheet, will be the operating table. The bedrooms will serve as recovery rooms, the beds as stretchers. Mother will stand by with cold water and fresh towels. The youngest boy will be operated on first. The older boys will serve as orderlies and remove him to the bedroom. The next youngest will be next, and so on up the line.

"When it comes to the last and oldest boy," Doctor Osler said, "he's too heavy to carry and there's nobody left to carry him. We'll leave him to recover on the operating table. Now, are there any questions on procedure?" No questions were raised. He turned his attention to the patients.

While Doctor Osler was reconnoitering and planning procedure, Doctor Bailey was bantering with the brothers, allaying our fears, and gaining our confidence. At the outset we stood unobtrusively in the background, attentive and well washed, particularly in the face, neck, and ears region. By the time Doctor Osler focused on us we were lounging at ease, at peace with the world.

"Madam," Doctor Osler began, "the arrangement you made was for five operations, but I see six boys here. Was one of them born without tonsils?"

"No," Mother replied. "we lived in Provo last year so Dave could start college. The boys have sore throats every winter. Last year Cy's tonsils got so bad that we had them taken out. He's had no trouble since. That's why we decided to have the other boys taken care of this summer, before they get infected again."

Doctor Osler examined all of his patients before turning to me. He looked casually at my throat, then examined it carefully. "Hmmm. a nice job, lad, excellent job. Tell me all about it."

Having been salved into a talkative mood by Doctor Bailey, I relished the invitation to move front stage center. Rule one in our house was: Talk as long as you wish, but when you have to stop for breath you lose the floor. I was primed for the chance to ignore this restriction.

"My doctor had examined me in advance, so he was ready to go to work as soon as I got settled in his fancy barber chair," I began. "Good thing. I didn't have time to get scared before he took a monstrous needle to me. He gave me a chance to catch my breath, then came at me again: one, two, three more times. I started to wonder about the wisdom in all this.

"After a bit, though, when things got numb, he started snipping around in there with a delicate looking paring knife that he called a scalpel. Occasionally he'd shove a pair of scissors into my mouth -- special scissors that were spring-loaded to keep 'em closed. I figured he was clamping off the vessels to stop the bleeding.

"By and by he pulled out a gadget with a wire noose on the end. It looked like a miniature rabbit snare, and a dandy design at that. Well, he must have put that noose right at the neck of the tonsil because as he drew it tight, snap went the tonsil. The first one came out pretty slick but by then my mouth was so full of scissors he could hardly navigate."

At this point Doctor Osler looked hard at his watch. Hmmm, I wondered, maybe I'm taking advantage of my chance to be in the limelight. I guess I'd better close it off.

"Eventually," I ended my speech, "he got the second one and sat back to take a rest and give the scissors time to seal the blood vessels. In due time he removed all the scissors, told me to eat nothing but soft foods for a couple of days, and released me. I had a double-decker ice cream cone on the way home and a malted milk when I got there. That's all there was to it."

"That was a vivid description, lad," Doctor Osler said, as he turned to address the others. "Boys, he was a good patient, and I'm sure you'll be good patients, too. There's a difference between his operation and yours. His was a local. You'll be under general anaesthetic. He was conscious during the surgery and had some pain and discomfort. You'll be temporarily unconscious and will feel nothing. You're more fortunate than he in that respect. Yet after the operation he suffered only the problem of healing. You will have, in addition, a headache and nausea from the ether. You'll be sick for a while, but it'll pass, certainly by morning. Now for the first patient."

Jack, the youngest, hesitated a moment then strode forward, pale but with a forced smile on his seven-year-old face. Doctor Bailey, with a reassuring touch to the shoulder, took command.

"Jack, my boy, when I give the word, position yourself comfortably supine on the table."

Jack's eyes opened wide with a mixture of concern and questioning.

"Don't be afraid of a strange word like that, Jack, it's just a fancy way to say, "lying face up." I have to have you face up because I'm going to place a cloth, saturated with ether, over your nose, and ask you to breathe normally. Soon you'll be asleep as in a dream. At the right moment I'll change to a whiff of chloroform. That's to make sure you stay asleep until we finish the operation."

"How long is this going to take, Doctor Bailey?"

"Just a little while, and when it's over your brothers will put you to bed and make sure you're recumbent. That's a fancy way to say, 'lying down comfortably.' Now, up on the table with you, Jack, and don't forget those big words. When school starts and you tell the teacher about your operation she'll be surprised and pleased with all the things you've learned this summer. All right, Jack?"

Jack, in willing response to Doctor Bailey's instruction, leavened with subtle diversion, climbed into position. Doctor Bailey administered the anaesthetic and monitored the patient. Doctor Osler performed the operation. The orderlies transferred the patient to his recovery room. The surgeon said, "Next."

The next volunteer was Wayne, age ten. With a smile as big as a fourth-quarter moon, he hopped on the table and said, "ready."

Doctor Bailey, wishing to show appreciation for the responsive disposition of this lad, but directing his comments for the benefit of the others, said, "Wayne, I'm proud of you and pleased with your attitude. Jack was a good patient and in short order will be recovering. You are a good patient, too, and a good example for your older brothers. Now up on the table with you, and we'll go to work."

Things were moving along smoothly, altogether too smoothly. The next patient was Dick, at age twelve a man to be

31

reckoned with. He marched forward with a simple declaration: "Let's get it over with."

Doctor Bailey was taken aback momentarily, although from his earlier banter with us he had a premonition that if a problem were to develop it would be with this one. "Richard, my boy," he said, "the success of our operation depends largely upon the attitude of the patient. We can do a good job for you only if you cooperate willingly with us. If you resent us, you'll resist the anaesthetic, and in your subconscious state create problems both for yourself and for us.

"Richard, I'm not going to knock the chip off your shoulder that says let's get it over with, because that's not what we want to do. We want to do this right. We want you to heal properly. Most of all we want you, when you're well, to be that great little guy that I knew you'd be when I helped your mother bring you into this world."

Dick the stoic, the boy who considered himself a man, relaxed. The pugnacious chin retracted, the scowl softened, the heart melted. He said, "Doctor, you're right," and submitted gracefully. With Dick's operation complete, there were three down and two to go.

Next on the schedule was Marlin. He was too smart to raise a ruckus, and at seventeen too old to be treated lightly. He approached this ordeal as he approached all challenges, with due deliberation. He had chosen to submit, and in submission would do the right thing: relax. In addition, he was determined, as one in a family of competitive brothers, not to be shown up by his juniors. He wasn't shown up. He was an ideal patient. That left only Dave, at nineteen the oldest.

Doctor Osler was ready to proceed, but Doctor Bailey demurred. "Dave," he said, "I want you to know that all of you boys will be sick little pups when you come out of the ether. Your younger brothers will need a leader to follow. I know that your parents will join me in expecting you to set an example for them. Are you with me, Dave?"

"Yes sir, Doctor Bailey," Dave said. That was all that needed to be said. His eyes expressed the rest.

Five up. Five down. Mission accomplished.

On the following Saturday upper-town met lower-town in the scheduled ball game. No forfeit was necessary. The throats were healed, and all players were eager to play ball.

A few months later our father received a bill:

"David Osler, M.D., and Steele Bailey, Jr., M.D.
"Five tonsillectomies performed @ $10.00 each.
"Charges – $50.00"

# Chapter 5

# Fading of Youth

The transition from boyhood to manhood was normally a rewarding experience for mining camp kids. Those of us who matured during the approach of the Great Depression, however, enjoyed no such transition. We had no youth. We were boys, then suddenly men.

The happy hours after school, on weekends, and throughout the summer season were rudely changed from times of play to times of work. With the irrepressible optimism of youth, we believed that play and work were not mutually exclusive. Our attitude was that if we must work, let's get some fun out of it.

As the impact of the Great Depression deepened, we faced the realities of a man's world. There was scant room for fun, and the workplace became increasingly hostile. We found that the experience we had gained as boys doing men's work was invaluable in entering that hostile workplace. One lesson we learned was that If a nasty job has to be done, don't back off, put some muscle into it.

\*   \*   \*   \*

Roy Lazzenbee was an enterprising rancher. One day he said, "Cy, breakin' wild hosses puts bread and potatoes on the table, but that's about all. I'm going to try somethin' to add a little gravy. Besides, I don't like to be called a mustanger. Some of these guys kill wild hosses to sell as pet food. Others kill 'em from airplanes to preserve forage for their livestock. This brings the job of mustangin' under a cloud and I don't like it. I'm going to add some pens and corrals for shearing sheep as the herds come through. Do you want a job trompin' wool at two bucks a day?"

"I sure do." It was great fun to help on the roundup of wild horses and ride mustangs, but there was no money in that. Any young fellow likes to see a dollar or two once in a while.

Roy built a substantial tripod topped with a steel ring to support a burlap bag. On one leg of the tripod he nailed cleats so the tromper could climb to the top and jump into the partially filled bag. When the shearing season arrived, he approached me.

"Cy, the Okelberry herd will be trailing through in a day or two. Now here's the deal: Wool is bulky. To make it handy for shipping, we compact it in burlap bags. They're about three and a half feet in diameter by seven feet long. The tripod supports the bag while it's being filled. Your job is to stomp it down as the shearers toss the fleeces into it. You got it?"

The herd trailed in, and the shearers arrived. Roy showed me how to clamp the open end of a bag to the ring, and we went to work. As each of the four shearers finished shearing a sheep, he folded the fleece inside out, tied it together with a straw string, and tossed it into the bag as would a basketball player shooting for the hoop.

Normal shearing practice is to stuff on the inside of the fleece anything that contributes to weight. This includes all dung, whether hardened or fresh, regardless of the sensitivities of the tromper confined in the burlap bag.

As the fleeces accumulated I climbed the tripod, jumped down into the bag, and tromped, tromped, tromped to compact the wool. While I was tromping, additional fleeces dropped down on my head, showering the contents on and about me.

**Tromping Wool**

36

Roy could see that I didn't relish having sheep dung in my hair and eyes. He gave me the facts: "Cy, you were hired to tromp wool, not to complain about sheep shit. And you oughta know that wool is sold by the pound, and every pound counts."

At the end of the day I was coated with raw lanolin, covered with sheep shit, and ready for a bath. Roy said, "Don't take a bath. That wool grease is good protection. You better daub yourself with turpentine to keep the wood ticks at bay." So I stripped and gave myself a turpentine sponge bath from scalp to toes, with assistance from him on places I couldn't reach.

By the end of the job I had tromped three thousand fleeces into seventy bags. I was eighteen dollars richer, and ready to get back to the fun of riding half wild mustangs for free.

\*　　\*　　\*　　\*

One day in the summer of 1926, Stewart Allen and I found ourselves broke. It's no fun to be broke when you're twelve years old and Tom Mix is showing at the movie house.

Stewart came from the wealthiest family in town. His father was Resident Manager of the mines in the area. His salary was widely known to be $333.33 per month. He was "careful with his money" and didn't squander it on childrens' allowances. Stewart had to scrounge for spending money like all the other kids in town. His claim to fame lay not in himself, but in his sister Maurine and his brother Harlow.

Maurine wore short skirts, high heels, and lots of perfume. That combination attracted the boys and drew envy from the girls. A rumor was floated that Maurine wore perfume rather than take a bath. That seemed unlikely, as the Allen residence was equipped with a bathroom. When the rumor reached Maurine, she quit wearing perfume but still wore short skirts and high heels. She continued to attract the boys.

Harlow was the town hero, the fullback on the high school football team, and a real bruiser. Usually when fisticuffs appeared imminent among the small fry, an argument would erupt. The smaller contestant would say, "Maybe you can lick me, but my brother can lick you." The other would say, "Yes, but my older brother can lick him." On up the line the argument would go. In any such duel of wits, Stewart was the winner. He could always bring into play his brother Harlow, and that was that!

The Allen family lived rent-free in the grandest house in town. In addition to its bathroom, it was equipped with a furnace for central heating. To raise the temperature throughout the house, they had only to open the draft or shovel in more coal. That was luxury living in a western mining town.

Most families survived on miner's wages of $5.00 a day, which was spent on the necessities of life. There were few luxuries. Poppa made home brew. Mamma made root beer. Children dug sego lily bulbs, and roasted pine nuts as special treats. Houses were heated by the kitchen range. During cold weather large rocks were heated in the oven and tucked in the blankets. Children slept two, sometimes three, in a bed.

One might have expected that Stewart would be cocky and spoiled from living in relative splendor, but he was not. He was a regular guy – skinny, freckled, and a great buddy.

One summer day Stew and I considered our situation. We rummaged the town dump and salvaged a wheelbarrow load of scrap iron. We reckoned it might bring us four-bits, but the junk man wasn't due till Wednesday.

"Let's figure another way to get into the picture show," I suggested.

"I've got it," Stew said. "We've collected a lot of Mason jar lids that are worth a penny apiece for the zinc. Maybe we can peddle twenty five of them to Mac Bigler for twenty cents. He'll have a nickel profit when he sells 'em to the junk man next Wednesday. If he goes for our deal, we can take in the Sunday matinee. Let's count on that. Now we've gotta figure out how we can make some real money. Maybe we can find a job digging cesspools."

Ernest Higginson's cesspool was pretty well filled up and he needed a new one. Most of the men in town dug their own cesspools, but Mr. Higginson was getting along in years. Besides, he had struck it rich on a lease at the Godiva Mine and didn't have to work. He told us he'd pay the standard rate of two dollars a foot, and showed us where to dig.

"How deep do you want her?"

"Go as deep as you can dig," he said. "Go all the way to China if you can."

We started with gusto, but soon found that the deeper we dug the harder it was to throw the dirt out of the hole. When we got down about five feet we reckoned we'd better reconnoiter if we were going to get anywhere near China. Besides, we took Mr. Higginson's crack as sort of a taunt and our dander was up. So we reconnoitered.

Almost anything can be found around an old mining camp if you know where to look. Kids who have all summer to prowl know all the best places. In short order Stewart and I scrounged an old windlass to use as a hoist, some scrap lumber to mount it, an ore bucket, and a piece of three-quarter-inch rope. We mounted the windlass on a crude framework and stapled one end of the rope to the drum, the other end to the bucket.

To guard against the drum slipping on the crank handle if there were too much weight in the bucket, we fashioned a safety brake independent of the handle. This safety feature, however, created another hazard. When the rope brake was used to lower the bucket, the crank handle swung round and round. If the operator didn't stand clear, he could get a whack on the head. Stew and I alternated between top man and shaft man. We made good progress until, at eighteen feet, we hit hard-pan that defied our best labors. We stopped to consider our situation. Eighteen feet will get us thirty six dollars. Maybe we can get a little more if we drill some holes and blast.

We scrounged some blasting powder, caps, and fuse, then "borrowed" some drill steel and a hammer from Pappy's shop. We drilled five holes about three feet deep. When we were ready to blast, Stew manned the windlass and I loaded the holes with blasting powder.

I crimped blasting caps onto the fuses, laced each into a stick of blasting powder, and tamped each charge into a hole with a cover of dirt. I checked to see that Stew was ready, split the free end of the fuses, and called out "Ready to fire!"

"Let her rip!" Stew responded.

I "spit" the fuses with my carbide lamp and yelled, "Man aboard. Take her away!"

I climbed on the bucket and was drawn up the shaft as Stew cranked the windlass. About half way to the top my upward movement slowed, then stopped. I started to inch downward, then wham! I dropped to the bottom.

"Stew, what's the matter? Get me out of here. Stew!"

No response. No time to cut the fuses. I've got to get out of here. Quick! I scampered up the rope hand over hand. When I got to the top, there was Stew, flat on his back and conked out cold. I pulled him away from the shaft then boom! Soon there were four more booms.

**Stew KO'd by the windless handle**

When Stew regained his senses, I said, "What happened?"

"Well," he said, "I guess your weight plus the bucket was too much. The drum started to slip on the windlass rod and I reached for the brake. I was so scared I must have let go of the handle, because it came around and whacked me on top of my head. That's all I remember."

The next day we shoveled out the material loosened by our blasting, collected forty dollars from Mr. Higginson, and moved on to new ventures.

* * * *

Stewart was a valued friend. We shared many adventures and misadventures. We learned a lesson unloading railroad ties from a boxcar.

John Cronin was superintendent of the narrow-gauge railroad that hauled ore from the mines to the tipple at Silver City, where the ore was transferred from the narrow-gauge cars to the main line of the Denver & Rio Grande Railroad. One day in 1928 Mr. Cronin asked if I would like to take a contract moving a carload of ties from a boxcar on the Rio Grande track to a siding adjacent his narrow-gauge line. "Good performance at an attractive price," he said, "might lead to additional contracts as needs arise."

The idea of being a contractor for a man of Mr. Cronin's standing tickled my ego. Of course I would take the contract. To share my good fortune I offered my buddy Stewart full partnership in the deal. Stew had spent the summer at his uncle's farm and had sprouted five inches. Although as a man of fourteen I felt plenty able, I figured that a six-footer would come in handy removing ties from the upper tiers in the boxcar.

To determine an attractive price, we studied the situation. These ties were smaller than those used on main line railroads. They were six-by-six inch hemlock, about five feet long, and thirty or so pounds each. Fortunately for us, they were not impregnated with creosote or other preservative.

We built a ramp from the floor of the boxcar to ground level, removed the ties in the doorway, and made a time-and-motion study as the basis for quoting our price.

After limbering up by carrying a few ties to the siding, we noted the time on my Ingersol watch and started our study. With ready access to the ties in the boxcar, we lugged them, two at a time, for ten minutes. From that, we calculated the job at five hours of steady work. Figuring in our preparatory work and a

41

few five-minute breaks, it looked like one good day's work for two men. We told Mr. Cronin we'd do the job for ten dollars. That was satisfactory to him.

Early the next morning, with a gallon of water and four sandwiches each, Stew and I went to work. Each of us carried two ties at a time for about an hour. Our gait was slowing, so we took a break and sized things up. We had made good progress. Perhaps we didn't need to lug two at a time.

With neither of us proposing but both of us agreeing, we started carrying the ties one at a time. This was a welcome change. and we lugged steadily until an early lunch break.

We had removed the ties from one end of the boxcar and half the doorway. We still had a long day ahead of us, so after a quick lunch we resumed the task. By two o'clock our pace had slowed to a sluggish walk, and thirty pounds seemed too much for one man to lug. So Stew took one end of a tie and I took the other. We removed the remaining ties in this fashion, and finished the job by six o'clock. We had learned at a tender age not to project a full-day performance from a ten-minute obsernation.

**Unloading ties was more work than reckoned**

\* \* \* \*

Work was scarce in Silver City, but was said to be plentiful at the mines in Pioche, Nevada. Scoop Simpson planned to hop a freight to Pioche and find out. My older brother Marlin and I decided to join him. We felt secure in tagging along with a professional railroader.

Scoop was about five-feet-two tall and four-feet-two around. His nickname derived from his prowess with a scoop shovel. As fireman on the local narrow-gauge railroad, he could shovel coal from the tender to the firebox of the locomotive at a remarkable rate. He was a bachelor, a sports addict, and a hero to the kids in town. Each year he bought football shoes for all the players on the local grammar school team.

Scoop, Marlin, and I walked to Tintic Junction, a station on the main line of the Union Pacific Railroad. We hopped a freight, and by late afternoon got to Caliente, Nevada, where a line branched off to Pioche.

Scoop and I crossed the Pioche railroad yards to get the lay of the land. Marlin tarried. When he started walking across the tracks, he was confronted by Caliente Red, the railroad detective. Red was widely known as a tough and ruthless bull. Marlin must not have shown proper respect. The bull uncorked a blow to the jaw which sent the poor kid sprawling.

"Get the hell outa this yard, and don't let me catch you again or I'll really let you have it!"

Marlin got the hell outa there and joined us. He and I decided that henceforth we would stay under the protection of Scoop.

At Pioche we went to the hiring office of the Pioche Consolidated mine. Scoop did the talking. "We're looking for work. Have you got a baseball team? I'm a hell of a good third baseman. I can work, too."

The man said, "We sure do have a ball team. Report for a tryout at four o'clock. If you're as good as you think you are, we'll find a job for you on day shift. You young fellers can go on the second shift at eight o'clock tonight. Here are chits you can use at the combination rooming-boarding house."

We checked in and had a good meal. Scoop left for baseball practice. Marlin and I joined a group of men loafing in the sunshine. We soon found ourselves chatting amiably with an old-timer who knew his way around.

"They hired us so quick," Marlin said, "we've been wondering. Work is scarce in the Tintic District. How come this camp is booming?"

"It's no secret," our new friend replied. "Pioche Consolidated is on its last legs. They're stripping all the ore they can get at the least cost. If the price of lead keeps dropping, they'll shut her down. It was a good hole to work in till they added a second shift. Now there is only four hours between shifts for the gases to clear out, instead of sixteen. She's about deep enough for me."

Our chat was interrupted as a magnificent Locomobile touring car moved up the narrow main street. It was occupied by seven of the most fetching bundles of feminine pulchritude my eyes had ever beheld.

"Look!" I said. "What in the world is that? I don't mean the car. I mean what's in the car."

"Oh, they're the girls from The House of Seven Gables. See that building on the hill with all the gingerbread? That's the fanciest whorehouse in the west. Each girl has a room with a gable. They parade up and down the street once or twice a day in that big Locomobile to advertise their wares. The driver is the madam. The one alongside is next in line. The three girls in the back seat have been around for a while, and the two on the jump seats are new to the game. Don't pay 'em a visit unless you've got a week's wages in your pocket. Don't have no more money on ya, cause no matter how much you've got, you'll come out broke."

It was nearly eight o'clock, so Marlin and I picked up our lunches and walked to the collar of the shaft with other men scheduled for the graveyard shift. The shaft had three compartments. One was a manway with air and water lines, and ladders for emergency exit. The other two were equipped with counterbalanced cages. The lowering of either cage assisted in raising the other. From all three compartments surged powder smoke and mine gases.

When our turn came, we joined six other men on one of the cages. As it dropped to each lower level, the air became more

44

and more oppressive. By the time the cage-tender let us off at the nine    hundred foot station we were sick. The shift boss could see it in our eyes. He took us to the face of the drift and said, "You can take turns mucking and tramming. Go easy to start. The gas'll settle down after a bit, and you'll be okay."

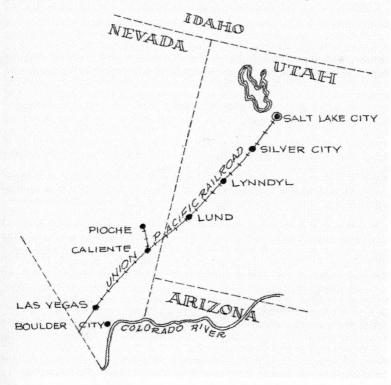

**Hobo route from Silver City, Utah to Pioche and Las Vegas, Nevada**

Marlin shoveled ore into the minecar. I pushed it along the track to the cager at the station, returned with an empty, and shoveled it full so Marlin could push that one out to the station. We alternated as muckers and trammers while the miner drilled a round of holes. Toward the end of the shift we helped lug his pneumatic drill and hoses to a secure place in the drift to protect them  during the next blast.

The miner loaded the holes with blasting powder and split the fuses. At precisely 3:45 A.M. he spit – that is, ignited – the fuses with his carbide lamp, and we cleared out. As we and other workers were raised to the surface, the roar of explosives reverberated through the mine.

Marlin and I recovered somewhat from our debilitating nausea, but headaches remained. We knew that in four hours the day crew would arrive to work in the smoke and gas that we just made, and that we would suffer the same fate when we come back. That is, if we do come back. No, we decided, the hell with it.

We slept off our headaches, had breakfast, and told the boss-man at the office, in true miner's vernacular, "she's deep enough for us." Scoop bade us farewell: "I made the ball team and got a day job. You guys watch your step." With that sound advice, we took a freight train south, made a wide circle around Caliente Red's railroad yard, and arrived in Las Vegas. We hoped to find day work and get a job in the sun.

Las Vegas had a population of about 3,500. We thought it was the hiring center of the "Big Six" combine of companies that was to build Hoover Dam. We found, however, that hiring was at Boulder City, a developing town near the dam site.

It was Saturday, and there would be no hiring until Monday. The only real chance for a job, we learned, was as high-scalers. Those were the men who, supported by a rope lifeline, pried and scaled loose rock and rubble from the walls of the dam site where concrete eventually would be poured. Marlin and I might not be good moles underground, but we were agile monkeys on the surface. We decided that next Monday we'd hire out as high-scalers.

Having a day and a half to kill, we explored the town. As the evening progressed, we made friends with an elderly barmaid at one of the saloon/gambling houses. She was the motherly sort, a handsome woman who must have been a striking beauty in her prime. An immediate bond developed as we confided our situation. She suggested how we might best spend our time in Las Vegas.

"It's nice weather," she said. "You might sleep in the park if you can get away with it. The park is patrolled by both the local cops and the railroad bull. They don't like bums hanging around. Excuse me, I didn't mean that. They try to reserve it for children. Maybe you can catch a few winks late at night. You can entertain yourselves for a few hours by going down to Block Sixteen, and later hide out at the park."

"What's Block Sixteen?"

"I don't mean to pollute you, but Block Sixteen is our whorehouse row, a good place for young fellows to get an education. From the far side of the street, that is."

She told us how to get there, and continued her story. "The girls put on their best show on Saturday nights. That's when the single bucks are on the prowl, and the cowboys hit town for a spree. Each hooker has her private parlor house. Sometimes it's just a booth, but it always has a roof that extends out over the sidewalk. As the guys walk down from town, usually loaded with booze, the fun is to see how far they'll get before they succumb.

"The old hookers and the least attractive have their quarters nearest town. They get first crack at the customers. The farther a guy can get, stumbling down Block Sixteen, the more amorous he becomes and the more attractive he finds the girls. If he can get near the far end of the line, I must say, he finds some pretty attractive stuff. You go find out for yourselves – from the far side of the street, mind you."

We followed her instructions. From the far side of the street, we watched the men – old, young, drunk, sober – wend their way down Block Sixteen. We had fun trying to guess how far particular individuals could make it before entering one of the "entertainment centers." We had difficulty controlling our imagination, but no problem in restraining our urges. We were broke. By two o'clock in the morning, tired of being on the fringes of life, we meandered to the park.

It was well patrolled. We had no chance to find an unguarded sleeping place, so we walked the town until daybreak. We had a breakfast of day-old cookies, and decided we were safe in taking a nap in the shade of one of the park trees. We were soon fast asleep. As the sun moved across the sky, we were out of the shade. When Marlin awakened he found me with the sun bearing full on my face. He roused me.

"My God, Marlin, what's wrong? I can't open my eyes!"

My lids were sunburned shut. When I tried to open them, the pain was excruciating. We were frantic. Marlin sought help from our barmaid friend. The pharmacist she recommended was sympathetic. He coated my eyelids with salve and bandaged them closed. "Just leave them covered for a few days, and give them frequent applications of this salve," he said.

Marlin led me as a blind man to the railroad yard to catch a freight. We were intercepted by the bull. Marlin blurted out our problem.

"Ha," the bull said. "That's the goddamndest story I ever heard. Get the hell outta this yard, or I'll run ya in."

We got the hell out of his yard and managed to evade surveillance in boarding a boxcar headed for home. Somehow our car escaped the attention of Caliente Red, and we returned to Tintic Junction, then Silver City.

We dreaded explaining to our parents the circumstance of my plight. We had left home ostensibly to help an uncle on his farm. That story wouldn't stand up. Luckily we had a friend whose parents hid us out for a few days until my eyelids healed. We then hitchhiked down to the farm for another few days. When we returned home we could truthfully say that we had been helping our uncle put up his hay.

\* \* \* \*

Tragedy struck our family in the summer of 1928. Late at night the house next door caught fire. The blaze jumped to our house and it burned to the ground. All my boyhood treasures went up in smoke. What remained of my youth faded with them.

Although my parents maintained a stoic exterior for the benefit of their boys, they must have wept inside at their loss. When they bought that house in 1923 they announced proudly,

48

"No more living on the wrong side of the tracks. We're moving to upper-town."

We were delighted. No more studying under the light of a coal oil lamp. No more pumping water from a well. No more outside toilet. We were going to have electricity and maybe a telephone. We'll have water out of a tap and an inside bathroom. We had arrived!

Mother made a home out of that house. She made curtains and doilies and things like that. She planted some rhubarb and pruned the morning glories. Father installed a picket fence between the house and the road. He hired "Painter Peterson," the finest mixer of white-lead paint in town, to do the painting. The best was none too good.

Our house was in the better part of town, where all the neighbors took pride in their surroundings. Over the years, however, the adjoining house deteriorated. Perry Dodge, the owner, was unable to keep up appearances. He was suffering from miner's consumption and not expected to live. My father planned, at the proper time, to buy it and tear it down.

At the time of the fire I was helping an uncle at his farm. A few days later I learned the details of the catastrophe from my brother Dave. "Perry Dodge died and Hazel was left destitute. To drown her sorrows she took to the bottle and got mixed up with Bobby Steele. One night they got a bright idea and set fire to her house for the insurance. Our house went with it.

"Pappy could sympathize with Hazel. She had three kids to think about, so he didn't make a big fuss about it. The next time he saw Bobby Steele, however, he damn near beat poor Bobby to a pulp. If he'd known the plan in advance he'd have had one of his trucks ready with a long cable. He could have pulled Hazel's house onto the street before ours caught on fire."

Dave's report of our loss left me in an emotional quandary. I was too big to cry, but not big enough to control my grief. In an effort to hide it, I changed the subject. "Dave, you've got a dandy haircut for a change. Pappy must have been taking barber lessons."

"No," he said, "I was embarrassed to look like a shaggy dog one day and a shorn sheep the next, so I made a deal with Pappy. I told him, 'If each time I need a haircut you cough up four-bits, I'll get a professional job. In return I'll take over the job of shearing the other kids.' He said, 'That's a fair proposition.' So I've had a haircut by a real pro. To make you fellows happy I'll do my best to learn the barbering trade. Judging from your Dutch cut, I'll have plenty of practice."

# Chapter 6

# Coping with Reality

In 1928 the town of Silver City was threatened with disaster. The narrow-gauge railroad that hauled ore from the mines to the main line of the Denver & Rio Grande Railroad was to shut down. The mines had no other means of transport and would have to fold. The neighboring town of Diamond was already a ghost camp. Only the cemetery remained. Unmarked graves, overgrown with gnarled and twisted sagebrush, provided stark testimony to the former existence of this once thriving town. Silver City now faced a similar fate unless some way were found to save the narrow-gauge railroad.

Silver City had had its ups and downs ever since the Sunbeam lode was discovered. Fires and flash floods, strikes and cave-ins, epidemics of smallpox and typhoid fever; it had weathered them all. Now metal prices have slumped, and some of the mines have shut down. What will happen if they all shut down? On reduced tonnage the railroad can't operate a big locomotive with a full train crew. My father thought he could build a gasoline powered locomotive. Its two-man crew could handle one carload at a time and work as many hours as necessary to take care of production at the mines. My father was a division boss for the State Highway Commission. His trucks had been manufactured for the army during the Great War by Packard, Nash, and Pierce-Arrow. Clint Parcel, his heavy equipment mechanic, kept those trucks in repair. Clint was exceptionally able and ingenious, a thinking man who was a doer. He called my father "Super," short for superintendent.

"Clint," Super said, as they were thinking about becoming railroaders, "you remember that fire at the warehouse of the Eagle & Bluebell mine? They've got a hell of a lot of equipment there that they figure is just scrap. Maybe we can salvage some of it. Let's drive over and take a look."

The thing that first drew Super's attention was the chassis of an underground locomotive. The electric motor and accessories had been burned, but the heavy frame and wheels were sound. "Clint," Super said, "the track width on this rig is the same as on the narrow-gauge railroad. We live right. All we need is a power plant."

"Super, I've found the answer to a mechanic's prayer. The boss had his Peerless car in here, and she's burned to the ground. I'm sure the motor and transmission can be cleaned tip-top. We can damn well find a radiator and patch up what has to be patched. She's got a rugged old V-8 engine. As I recall, it has a three and a quarter bore, and a five inch stroke. We can tie the transmission in series with the locomotive gearing and run our train any speed we want."

Super and Clint approached John Cronin, superintendent of the railroad, for a lease. "Sure enough," Mr. Cronin said, "the railroad is tied in with the mines, and we're so eager to keep the mines going we'll give you a no-royalty lease and full use of our shop to boot."

With their lease in hand, the partners bought the locomotive and the Peerless car, quit their jobs, and went to work. Soon they had their rig rolling. Business was good. To keep up with demand they had to run day and night. To provide a two-man crew and have a responsible man on the throttle at all time, Super and Clint alternated as engineer. Dave, Marlin, or I served as the second hand. The second hand was a factotum -- brakeman, switchman, errand-runner, whatever was required.

Business flourished, the partners prospered, and a substantial reserve accumulated in their bank account. "Clint," Super said one day, "this working around the clock is getting to be too much of a good thing. The Salt Lake Junk Company has some narrow-gauge locomotives that were made for the army during the Great War. Each one'll weigh about ten tons and should be able to pull three cars at a time. If we bought one and fixed it up we could get our work schedule down to a decent eight hour day."

"That's a good idea. Let's take a look." They took a look, bought and reconditioned a ten-ton locomotive, and soon had it running ship-shape. The work day shrank from 24 to eight hours. That was good for the partners and good for the boys, as school would soon begin.

Things were looking up. Then disaster struck. The mines still operating reduced their output. Within a few months the last of the mines served by the railroad closed down. That was the end of one venture. Perhaps a new start could be found in a forthcoming celebration. There is nothing like a celebration to raise the spirits.

*　　*　　*　　*

The Tintic Silver Jubilee was staged at Eureka to commemorate the sixtieth anniversary of the discovery of rich mineral deposits in the Tintic Mining District. As planned, this extravaganza memorialized the good times of the past. Not as planned, it presaged the bad times of the future. For the Tintic Mining District this was the last big blast before the onslaught of the Great Depression. It was held August 28, 1929.

Eureka was a wide open town except when the government agents, the G-men, were around. In the saloons, bootleg liquor was slid along the bar at two-bits a shot. The sheriff looked the other way. Otherwise he wouldn't be sheriff. He agreed, at the urging of compatriots, to allow open gambling for this one-time celebration. Enforcement of the law was subordinate to the allegiance he felt toward his voting constituents.

Town officials, union leaders, bootleggers, and madams joined with saloon keepers and other merchants to form a Jubilee Committee. The committee contracted with gamblers from Las Vegas to provide gaming tables and serve as dealers. Roulette, Faro, and Black Jack were apportioned among the saloons and pool halls. The committee raised $25,000 as seed money to underwrite the gambling venture. Mine managers declared a holiday from Wednesday through the weekend. It was Big Time.

A baseball game was played at the high school athletic field, followed by contests to determine the champions in rock drilling, shoveling, and weight lifting. A horseshoe tournament was held at one section of the playing field, boxing contests at another, and foot races at center stage. Money prizes were awarded to all winners.

In advance of this big event, my father, with a twinkle, had told me how to train for the races. "First," he said, "practice running with sheet-lead innersoles in your shoes. Take them out just before the race. Second, rub angle-worm oil into your knees. It's a marvelous lubricant that will penetrate all the way into your joints. Collect the oil this way: Punch a hole in the bottom of a coffee can. Half fill the can with sand. Toss in a handful of angle-worms and cover the top with glass. Put the can on the window sill in the kitchen where it's hot. As the worms melt, their oil will filter through the sand. Collect it from the hole in the bottom of the can and store it in the icebox. Label it or your mother might have a surprise."

I won the race in my age group. Whether my victory was the result of following the prescribed training regimen or my natural ability was a matter to ponder. However, I didn't ponder the spending of my winnings. For two-bits apiece I had banana splits and ice cream sodas galore. Those delicacies were normally enjoyed only on July Fourth.

After the celebration the committee met to count the proceeds from its gambling venture, and distribute the winnings among the providers of seed money. Surprise! There were no winnings. Only a pittance remained of the $25,000 provided as start-up money.

"How could that be?" Adolph Atherly said. "There should be winnings. I don't know anybody who won more than a few dollars. There were only three fellows -- I didn't know them -- who were winning regularly. I don't see how they could have broken the bank. Hmmm, now I just wonder."

"Quit your wondering," Carl Galloway said. "I noticed those same three guys. They must have been in cahoots with the gamblers. The dealers swished them money they didn't win, and we weren't smart enough to know it. That's your answer. That's how they took us."

The promoters of the Jubilee accepted their loss and chalked it up as a lesson well learned. The miners of the district, unemployed in increasing numbers as the Great Depression worsened, learned lessons too, bitter lessons in survival. They cut fence posts from the cedar trees on the surrounding hills to trade with farmers for basic foodstuff. They forsook their role as hard-rock miners – king-pins of the industry by their own definition – to work in coal mines for their fuel. Their efforts, although noble, proved inadequate. Many of their children were undernourished. The Red Cross set up kitchens in the schools, and provided hot cereal and soup for sustenance.

* * * *

The future for young adults was bleak. Brother Marlin graduated from high school in 1930. Knowing that college for him was only a dream for the indefinite future, he decided to join the Navy. If he got through boot camp perhaps he could qualify for one of the Navy schools. He needn't have worried about his ability to pass any qualifying examination that came along. He had a remarkable memory upon which to draw. He had developed that memory through association with Theo B. Miller, a former professor of speech.

Mr. Miller had been a specialist in speech disorders at a large midwestern university. His wife ran away with another faculty member. Neither bothered to get a divorce. Professor Miller and the wife of the other professor decided to make the best of it and share their lives. In this scandalous circumstance he resigned, and with his consort moved to her home town of Eureka, Utah. They started a nursery and floral business. He advertised in the *Eureka Reporter* that he could correct stuttering and stammering disorders. "Only persons willing to follow strict discipline need apply," he stated.

Marlin had suffered a serious stuttering defect almost from the time he could talk. From mimicking him, I had a similar but lesser problem. We knew that persons who stutter can sing, so we tried talking in sing-song fashion. That was more embarrassing than stuttering. We tried swinging our arms back and forth to create a speaking rhythm. That didn't help, so Mother took us to see Professor Miller.

After examining us thoroughly, Mr. Miller said, "Boys, your problem is posture. Your angel wings protrude more than they should. There is an abnormal hollow between your shoulders and your buttocks. Your diaphragm is weak, so when you talk there isn't proper air flow from your lungs. If you stand erect with chest high, your shoulders will straighten up. I can give you physical exercises to correct your posture and phonic exercises to correct your speech. However, I won't bother with you if you are not prepared to work, work, work."

We were prepared to work. We did work, and within a month I could, and did, talk, talk, talk. Professor Miller released me, with the admonition, "continue exercising, especially in voicing with full lungs and a deep voice the vowel sounds A-E-I-O-U."

Marlin continued his regimen. To display his improvement, he read passages that struck his fancy to Mr. Miller. To better his performance he memorized those passages, then whole paragraphs. By the time his stuttering was cured, he had developed such interest in dramatics that he continued his "studies in elocution" under the tutelage of Professor Miller. In furthering those studies he acquired an ability to memorize and retain a vast amount of information simply by reading it three or four times. He felt he could pass any examination the Navy might present.

Marlin joined the Navy, survived boot camp, passed the test for a Navy school, and after nine months of study graduated from the Machinist's Mate school at Norfolk, Virginia. He was assigned duty on a heavy cruiser, the USS *Marblehead*. Graduates of the school were given furloughs and expense money to travel to the home port of their ship. The home port of the *Marblehead* was the San Pedro/Long Beach Navy yard. Marlin propositioned four of his buddies who were also headed for California: "If you fellows will give me your travel allowances, I'll guarantee to get you there and you won't have to ride some damned old train either." His buddies agreed. With monies thus pooled, Marlin bought an automobile and drove the group to California. He was then proud owner of a 1926 Hudson Super Six sedan.

While at sea Marlin had no place to store his automobile. He wrote a letter home. "Dave, why don't you and Cy hitchhike down here. We'll have a little fun until my ship shoves off, then you can drive the old Hudson back home."

Dave and I were ready for a little fun. Rather than hitch the whole way, we hopped a freight train as far as Riverside, California, then thumbed the rest of the way to Long Beach. While waiting to be taken by launch to the USS *Marblehead*, we observed coming ashore a group dressed in the flashiest garb we had ever seen. I said to Dave, "Look, that must be the Navy Band." A sailor standing nearby nudged me, "Better be quiet, buddy, them guys are U.S. Marines." I kept quiet.

After spending a few days with Marlin, we were broke. "To get you fellows home," he volunteered, "we can hock my ring for gasoline money." His was a Navy signet ring with a large imitation ruby surrounded by seven small diamonds. The most we could get on a redeemable loan in a hockshop was five dollars. We took it. Marlin went to sea. Dave and I struck out for home.

"Let's figure this thing out," Dave said, as we started the trip. "We've got 700 miles to go. At fourteen miles to the gallon, we'll need fifty gallons. With gas at ten cents a gallon, we can make it."

A gas war was raging in California. As we drove through the suburbs of San Bernadino, we saw a sign at a filling station "gas -- 8.9 cents per gal, 3 cent tax included." A few miles farther along we saw a honey cannery that had burned. Five-gallon cans littered the yard. We helped ourselves to a dozen cans and drove back to the filling station. We filled the Hudson tank with gasoline, then filled cans until our money ran out. "We'd better fill one can with water," I suggested. "It might come in handy on the Nevada desert."

We drove homeward at a pretty good clip. When we refilled the gas tank from the cans, we calculated that our gas mileage was not up to expectations, so we kept a wary eye on the speedometer, and drove the old Hudson at thirty miles an hour except on downgrades. Then we speeded her up, kicked her out of gear, shut down the motor, and coasted to a near stop. Whether that strategy improved our mileage we didn't know, but it made us feel better.

After filling the gas tank on one occasion, we decided to add some water to the radiator. I smelled the cans. "Dave, where's the can with the water in it?" Dave smelled the cans. "My God, we've poured five gallons of water into the gas tank!"

**What? Water in the gas tank?**

We removed the plug from the tank and drained the contents into empty cans. Then we cut an empty can in half and decanted the mixture back and forth, losing hardly a quart of our precious gasoline. Eventually we arrived in Santaquin, Utah, about 25 miles from home, tired and hungry. At our grandmother's house we had a dandy cleanup campaign and a hearty meal. We drove to town to brag with friends about our happy experience. We didn't have a chance to brag. En route to town the Hudson ran out of gas. Perhaps that was a good way to bring our escapade to a close, and us back to reality.

*   *   *   *

Upon returning to Silver City, Dave and I found that the metals market, instead of recovering from a "temporary slump," had continued to plummet. Additional families had abandoned their homes for a fresh start elsewhere. Only the destitute and the optimistic remained. My father was among the last of the optimists to forsake this, his chosen town, for greener pastures.

As the depression worsened, Super realized that the railroad venture could not be revived. He had given it his best shot and failed. He had striven valiantly for a handle to cope with the reality of the depression. That coping handle had escaped him. He would try again.

With our house burned to the ground, the railroad venture a failure, and no future in Silver City, we loaded our furniture on Super's old Kissel truck and moved to Salt Lake City. It was July 23, 1931. That was a memorable day for Mother, in the anguish of expectation; for Father, in the quiet darkness of seeming defeat; for the brothers, each immersed in secret memories of the past and yearning hunger for the future.

For years my parents had scrimped and saved to invest fifty dollars each month in the Salt Lake Building & Loan Company. That "rock-solid company" filed for bankruptcy. My parents' share of its assets was their nest egg. With it they bought a large old house near the University of Utah.

"This house will be handy when the boys go to college," Mother reasoned. "Besides, with extra bedrooms we can always take in university students as roomers if times get really tough."

Times did get really tough. Father was always the optimist, and sometimes the gambler. Victim of unhappy circumstance that brought him as a stranger to the city, he found neither work for his aging frame nor challenge for his active mind. Bearing heavily the burden of his family's welfare, and finding no legitimate source of income, he chose bootlegging over welfare.

His old Studebaker, heavily laden with bootleg booze, blew a tire en route from the Tintic hills to the Cullen Hotel in Salt Lake City. The first passerby that stopped to lend a hand was, of all persons, deputy sheriff Bill Laird. The deputy did his duty. Pappy had gambled with the Volstead Act and lost. The judge ordered the contraband destroyed, and imposed the mandatory sentence for first offenders: six months in the county jail.

Total funds to maintain the family during Pappy's incarceration were twenty-two dollars per month. This was an allotment provided by Marlin, who knew the family plight. Mother's challenge was to maintain the house and to feed and clothe five boys on that amount. A problem arose when gas service was disconnected because we were two months in arrears. "I'll use a hot plate for cooking," Mother said. "We'll just have to do without hot water and take cold baths."

We knew that the cost of electricity would be prohibitive. An acquaintance, knowing our destitute condition, offered to share one of his "secrets of survival." He showed us how to stop the meter from recording without disturbing the flow of current to the house. "Now," he said, "check your past power bills and stop the meter so that the kilowatt-hours shown are about the same month after month. Make sure the meter isn't jimmied when the reader makes his rounds. Bear in mind this is larceny, so as soon as you get on your feet quit the tampering. Right?"

"Right."

Maintaining the supply of water required a different solution. When the men from the municipal water works arrived to disconnect the service, Dave confronted them with shovel raised and meaning clear: Close off that valve at your physical hazard! The foreman must have had some authority in matters of this nature. He arranged for Dave to work off our bill as a spare hand on his crew. Dave's labors were so favorably received that he was allowed to work off an estimated year's charges in advance, and our property taxes to boot.

How to keep the house warm the next winter? We knew the owner of an old dump truck that would be idle for a few days. We scouted the neighborhood, found persons willing to pay five dollars per ton for stoker coal delivered, and struck out for the mines in Carbon County. We could load coal at the mine for two dollars a ton and deliver it for five. We fulfilled the neighbors' requirements, delivered two loads in payment for use of the truck, and stashed away ten tons for our own use during the forthcoming winter.

Our physical security seemed secure, but the Great Depression was spreading like a malignant tumor, threatening all. Yet life was a shower of contrasts. To the young, the new school year opened wide the doors of promise. To their elders, all doors were closed and the future a mere extension of the past.

Dave had completed one year at Brigham Young University before our family finances collapsed. He longed to enroll at the University of Utah. However, he was working as a spare hand for the city. "I should be available for any work that turns up," he said. "If I were in school I might miss out on something. Besides, tuition costs twenty-one dollars a quarter. That's more than I can scare up."

The three youngest boys happily enrolled in the ninth, seventh, and fourth grades. They had explored Salt Lake City from the time we arrived until they started school: The sights, the sounds, the smells; the thoroughfares, the byways, the shortcuts – They knew them all. They knew throughout the city what every alley cat knows in its own back yard.

Without pocket money to spend, they had to scrounge for their fun. They found ways to breach the fence at the orchard behind the Holy Cross Hospital. They learned how to cajole the guards at the university stadium so they could watch football games for free. They made friends with the director of Victory Playground, who taught them, in his free time, how to play tennis. They were, in short, city kids ready to cope with city schools. They knew how to cope with reality.

As an incoming high school senior, I was in no sense city wise. I was timid and insecure in transferring from Tintic High

School at Eureka to one of the Salt Lake City schools. The graduating classes of Tintic High had fewer than half a hundred students while those of the city high schools had more than a thousand.

Salt Lake City had two major high schools. East High was located a few blocks from our house. West High was on the far side of the tracks about four miles away.

East High was the "Ivy League" school. Its students were drawn from the better areas of the city. West High was the cosmopolitan school. Its students came mostly from the working class, the foreign born, and those of all colors. It also drew students from upper crust households who preferred that their children be socially democratic.

When I went to East High School to register, I was ill at ease, confused, overwhelmed. I must have wandered into the wrong line, or otherwise committed some horrible sin. One of the teachers chastised me endlessly for not knowing what I was doing. I felt like the fool that she thought I was. I took her abuse to the limit of endurance then said, "Thank you for this exposure to East High School. Now excuse me. I'll go down to West High and register."

When I arrived at West High School, most of the students were registered and the desk was sparsely attended. As I entered the hall a large man came forward to greet me. "Did you ever play football, lad?" "Yes, sir, I played every quarter of every game in three years of high school."

"I knew it, lad, just looking at you," the man said. Roy A. McIntyre, head coach, led the way for my speedy registration. He and the other teachers studied my scholastic records. They bantered a bit to put me at ease in discussing my background, attitudes, and aspirations. When satisfied that I could cope, the committee arranged my schedule. It was not of snap courses geared to football players. It was of tough subjects taught by demanding teachers.

Roy McIntyre as a coach was interested in his boys as members of the football team. As a dedicated teacher he was

62

concerned for their total welfare. One day as the season advanced he took me aside.

"Cy, I know you can't afford to go on to the University. Why don't you try for Annapolis or West Point? Your athletic ability and scholastic record will help, but first you have to be top flight in competitive examinations on mathematics, English, and history. At the library there's a collection of the examinations used by the Service Academies over the past several years. If you study them you might come out on top."

I thanked him, and promptly began a systematic study of those examinations. The deeper I delved, the more evident it was that similar questions in each of the subjects recurred year after year. The questions were posed in various ways, but the subject matter, the essence of what was considered important, was clear. I decided to learn every facet of every question that recurred in those examinations. That study served me well in high school classes. It also gained me the top rank in the competitive examination for Annapolis, and an appointment to it by United States Senator Reed Smoot.

My appointment was conditional upon passing the physical examination. Final decision rested with the Annapolis Board. A preliminary exam by a local doctor was to weed out the unfit, thus save travel expense to Annapolis by candidates likely to be rejected.

Dr. John J. Galligan, the consulting doctor, hesitated upon seeing a scar on my forehead. He then examined me thoroughly. "Young man," he said, "I find you in perfect condition in all respects except one. I'm sorry to say that you'll never pass the Annapolis Board. That scar on your forehead will keep you out. Tell me, how did you get it?"

"I got it in a fight with my next older brother and he was the best man. When he gave me a wallop, I went head over heels out of the tail end of our father's pickup. We must have been going twenty miles an hour. I landed forehead first on the gravel road and slithered forward all the way to my crown. The doctors flushed out the wound with a mixture of gasoline and kerosene, then they sewed me up with catgut. The catgut disintegrated before the wound healed, so they had to sew me up again. That's why I have such a bad scar. Infection set in and my temperature soared.

"This happened in 1918. Fortunately, a nurse who had served in the World War volunteered to help my mother tend me. They kept me in iced sheets to keep my fever in check. Eventually I recovered and learned how to walk all over again. That happened when I was four years old, Doctor. I've taken a lot of tough knocks since then and that scar has never bothered me."

"I'm sorry, truly sorry, but I know what their reaction will be: Why should Annapolis accept someone who has a scar when there are thousands of young men to pick from who do not?"

Seeing my dejection, Dr. Galligan continued. "If you can raise fifty dollars to cover a week's stay in the hospital, I'll remove that scar surgically without charge. It will pass inspection in a couple of months."

"Doctor, it won't work. My class will begin before the surgery is healed. When the next class starts, I won't be eligible. If I can't go to Annapolis and be an admiral, I'll just have to attend the school of hard knocks. Thank you very much, Doctor." My voice failed as my dream vanished.

\* \* \* \*

Jim Myers had attended West High School a year earlier. When I enrolled as a greenhorn senior, he was an established Man-About-Town. Jim carried a slender frame to a height of six feet one. Most of the girls liked to look up to that height. Few of the boys could look down on it. His light complexion, delicate features, and infectious personality drew the girls to him. His warm smile, sincere friendliness, and drive to participate in the manly sports attracted the boys. His voice, pleasant when speaking and resonant when singing, added to his charm. He was truly a personality guy.

Jim drew me into his circle of friends and encouraged my participation in his many activities. As each of us gained from

64

qualities found in the other, our friendship ripened and our lives became closely intertwined. We shared our lunches. I enjoyed the store-bought goodies he carried in a brown lunch bag. He relished the sandwiches with homemade bread that I carried wrapped in newspaper. At our house we didn't have lunch bags. We couldn't afford them.

Jim had a working mother and two sisters. The Myers house was home to Jim because he lived there. It was a second home to me because of one of his sisters. It was a second home to another buddy because of the other sister. It was a rendezvous for all of us because one of the sisters had a part-time job. Some of the earnings from that job provided ingredients for making the home brew that enlivened our otherwise dull weekends.

Student streetcar tickets were available through the school system at two dollars for a packet of fifty. Jim and I had tickets, but we reserved them for emergency use. We walked the four miles to or from school to save the four cents.

Moleskin trousers were in vogue. Proper fashion was to wear them without laundering. The ultimate test of being "with it" was whether your pants could stand alone without slumping. Jim's could. Mine could.

I had two shirts that I wore on alternate days. One was a sleazy percale, a fifty-cent garment purchased on sale. The other was a quality broadcloth of ancient vintage, with garish brown stripes. I was embarrassed to wear either shirt, but had no choice. I had no other.

I was selected to give a speech at the high school graduation exercises. Mother helped me compose it. We both wondered what I would wear, standing before a thousand classmates and their proud parents. Dave took me in tow. At a fire sale we paid five dollars for a Society Brand suit. The conservative tan color was accented with a gaudy pattern that might have been popular with gamblers about 1910. The coat fit nicely. I didn't try on the pants, but discovered at home that the legs were so skinny they couldn't be drawn over my shoes.

Mother, ever alert to sensitivities, said, "I can fix that. You won't need the vest. I can salvage enough material from it to enlarge the pant legs." She tailored the pants, not in the popular bell-bottom fashion but the best she could. I gave my graduation speech and hastily withdrew through the stage exit to hide my embarrassment.

**Embarrassing moments in a "new" graduation suit**

I graduated from high school in the spring of 1932. Now what? My school year had been one of some embarrassment, more exultation, and considerable achievement. Embarrassment from poverty, a condition felt also by classmates and therefore not personal stigma to be dwelled upon. Exaltation from participating in school activities -- the play, the opera, and competitive sports. Achievement from inward drive leading not to public acclaim, but to personal satisfaction. I hoped that that drive would serve me as well in the world as it had in school. It was not to be.

Dave guided me into the ranks of the unemployed with scant encouragement. "I've applied for work at every conceivable place in this man's town," he said. "There's no work to be had. Even the employment agencies have shut down. The only chance we've got is to get out into the boondocks. Let's give it a whirl."

We did "give it a whirl." We scoured the countryside for work of any kind, at any wage. At mine and mill, farm and factory; in city, town and open range, no source of possible work escaped our probing. None bore fruit. An occasional temporary job provided sustenance and kept our hopes alive throughout the summer. We returned to our home in Salt Lake City for the winter, where Dave could fill in as a spare hand from time to time for the municipal water works.

In March, 1933, I had an opportunity to herd sheep. Good, I thought, this isn't a highfalutin' prospect, but it's a chance to get some steady work. I grabbed it.

In 1928 my father had bought part interest in a herd of sheep that his brothers owned jointly. The brothers were farmers who lived in nearby Santaquin. That was a convenient location between Pole Canyon, where they had summer grazing rights, and Keg Mountain in west central Utah, where they had winter rights. Their farms had stopover facilities for "lambing out" in the spring, as the herd was trailed from winter to summer grazing areas.

The expense of maintaining their herd of three thousand sheep was minimal. On the lush alpine pasture of the summer range only one herder was necessary. He did his own cooking. On the winter range both a herder and a campjack was required. Monthly wage for the herder was forty dollars and found; for the campjack, thirty. The "and found" part was for board and a bunk. The farmers provided most of the basic food from their own production. Their wives tossed in occasional delicacies from their cellar larders.

Annual income in recent years had averaged about three dollars per head for the wool crop in the spring and for the lamb crop in the fall. With sheep priced at sixteen dollars a head this promised to be a good investment. But what seemed a good investment in 1928 was soon a fiasco. Prices for wool and for lamb dropped so low that the combined return didn't pay the herd bill. In this sad state of affairs my Uncle Henry asked me one day: "Cy, wouldn't you like to help with the sheep for a month or so?"

"Sure, what's the deal?"

"We face this problem every year," he said. "Sheep have a memory like an elephant and they're stubborn as a mule. Every spring they remember the green grass on the summer range, and they can't wait to hit the trail back to it. Pretty soon we'll have to ride herd around the clock to keep them from trailing. We've got to give Art Wickman some help. Will you give us a hand? I figure it's worth fifteen dollars a month and found."

Having some knowledge of the contributions my uncles routinely made to the common cause, I could hardly refuse. And the money looked good. Next day Henry loaded some supplies in his Studebaker and drove me and my gear to the sheep camp on Keg Mountain. The camp was a Conestoga type wagon, modified with an automotive undercarriage and fitted with a trailer hitch. Henry "hitched on" and towed the camp about a mile to a site where the herd had fresh grazing and bedding areas.

The camp was wide enough to accommodate a double bed built crosswise at the rear, and positioned about three feet above the floor. Under the bed was a slot from which a table top could be drawn forward when in use and slid back when not required.

Benches were provided on both sides of the camp, convenient to the table top. Shelves and drawers were built in above. A sheet metal stove with a small oven stood in one corner near the door. Storage facilities, accessible from the outside, were available in the space at the rear of the camp, under the bed.

On the night that I arrived, Jason, the campjack, climbed into the far side of the bed. Art Wickman, the herder, said, "Cy, you hop in the middle. If the sheep start to trail I can roll out without disturbing you."

I was pleased to have Art on the outside. To have him roll over me would have been a distinct hazard. He was a man of substance, about 230 pounds of it on a five-foot-seven-inch frame. His chest, although massive, was eclipsed by his midsection girth. Evidently he enjoyed camp cooking.

I slithered under a quilt that seemed heavy as a mattress. When Art climbed in, the weight of that quilt and the body heat from heavy men on either side got to me. After a sleepless hour I extricated myself and spent that and all future nights on one of the benches, huddled in my sleeping bag.

When later I told Henry about the quilt, he explained: "Camp quilts are hard to clean. Every year Art's wife just adds an extra layer to them. Each layer is made of laundered denim from Art's worn-out overalls. That's why they're so heavy."

My first morning on the job was a pleasant introduction to life in a sheep camp. The crackling sound and pungent smell of sage brush burning in the sheet metal stove aroused me. Then the tantalizing aroma of coffee brewing in the pot and bacon frying in the pan got me up. The relentless cold of a desert night had succumbed to the warming glow of a desert day. The sun was high over the shadowy mountains to the east when Jason announced: "Hot cakes and eggs in five minutes, men. Come and get 'em while they're hot."

After a leisurely breakfast of Jason's sourdough pancakes, bacon and eggs, and numerous cups of coffee, Art called his dogs to heel and moseyed out to rouse the sheep. Camp life, it seemed, was a casual affair.

"Cy," he said, "when it's cold like this, sheep bed down so close together you'd think they might suffocate. They'd huddle there all day if I didn't kick 'em out."

As Art and his dogs roused the sheep to phlegmatic activity, I was due for a surprise: When three of the sheep didn't move, Art investigated.

"Bobcats!" he said. "They like brains. They jump on stragglers at the fringe of the herd. Sheep are defenseless. The cats go from one to another till they get their fill of brains. Coyotes, they're different. They like blood. They come underneath for the jugular, one after another, till they get their fill.

"Now these ones are fresh-killed, so we'll salvage some chops and dog meat, and skin 'em out. Pelts ain't worth much nowadays, but they're worth somethin." So we skinned them out. Art praised me a bit: "Bringing along your .25:20 carbine was a good idea. Never can tell when you'll run into one of the varmints."

As the day progressed, the warming sun brought the sheep to life and they scattered in all directions, browsing on the scant vegetation. Art moved to the northeast to turn back leaders that sought to trail for the summer range. He gave me some pointers on the art of herding sheep.

"We've got three thousand head and sixty of 'em are counters, the black-faced ones. If we want to see if we've lost part of the herd, we count the counters. If we don't have sixty, we go lookin' for the rest.

"We've got about forty head with bells. We put bells on the trouble makers, the ones we know want to head for some place we don't want 'em to go. Then the others follow. Sheep are stubborn critters. If you drive 'em forward they go backward. If you drive 'em backward they go forward. And one thing's for sure. If one of 'em strikes out for the summer range, they all follow."

Art had four dogs that worked for him. Occasionally he rode one of the horses. Usually he walked or sat on a perch while his dogs, on verbal or whistled command, kept the herd under control. He tried to get two of his dogs to work with me. He ignored them. He paddled them. He starved them and had me feed them. His efforts were unsuccessful; his dogs wouldn't change allegiance.

I worked long and hard, walking or riding back and forth to control the herd. Without a dog to run for me, my best efforts were ineffective. I sensed that I was not holding up my end.

As lambing time grew near we began trailing the herd toward the summer range. The start of our migration served as a signal to the sheep of better things to come. Restive before, they were now impatient to move on, and doubly difficult to control.

The strain of responsibility weighed heavily on Art. One evening I told him to relax and have a good sleep; I would control the herd that night. I did control it, walking or riding back and forth until about three in the morning. Exhausted, I decided to sit for a few minutes with my back to a juniper and my face to the herd.

With a start I woke up at daybreak. Bells were tinkling in the distance and not a sheep was in sight. The entire herd had trailed right over me.

I galloped toward the source of the sound and there found Art and his dogs in total control. His instincts were better than my noble intentions. "Art," I said, "I'm awful sorry."

"That's all right," he replied, "I had a better rest than I figured on."

I didn't know whether this was a putdown or a compliment. I took it on the bright side, as a helper who had, although in failure, given his best.

We had brief respite at a stopover where the sheep were shorn. The Union Pacific Railroad had provided a rail siding, with pens and corrals, for shearing the numerous herds that trailed through from winter to summer grazing ranges. As the shearing of one herd was finished, another herd moved in. Transient shearers, wranglers, and roustabouts moved the sheep through pens and shearing stations in prompt order.

Art heaved a sigh of relief: "This is a good operation. The railroad gets the freight. Shearers get some work. We get a rest. You can't beat that."

The sheep were gaunt from their winter ordeal and heavy with lamb. However, being relieved of their wool and released from confining corrals, they now trailed with renewed vigor. But Art and I, rested and buoyed knowing that home was near, retained control. At the end of the trail we were met on the outskirts of Santaquin by my father's three brothers. There we separated the herd into four bands. Each brother was to lamb out a band, and another man and I were to lamb out the fourth.

The other man was Harold Kay, a rugged young farmer whose handling of sheep was highly regarded. Harold was not an intellectual by any means. He was about as deep as a pie plate. But he had common sense in a practical sort of way. His first comment to me was, "Cy, herding sheep is like trying to saddle a cow. You work like hell but what's the point? Sometimes I can't figure it out".

After we got settled into the camp he looked over our band with a contemplative eye. "Not many dry ewes here," he observed. "They must have been knocked up pretty good. As good, by golly, as if I'd had a hand in it myself."

Harold knew the habits of sheep. As he sensed my vast ignorance, he filled in some of the gaps in my understanding of barnyard lore.

"It looks like we'll lamb out at a hundred percent, that's a lamb for every ewe in the herd," he said. "The yearlings normally have one lamb. The two-to four-year-olds have twins. The five-year-olds have one lamb, and if they don't continue to produce we sell 'em for mutton. If we get enough twins to make up for the losses, we get that hundred percent.

"We sell the wether lambs, the castrated males, for a cash crop in the fall, and hold the ewes to replenish the herd. To control when the lambs are born, we keep the bucks in separate ram-pasture. Last fall we turned 'em loose to the herd two weeks early to get a few extra pounds on the lambs before sending 'em to early market. If we get bad weather we lose more than we gain. That's the chance we take."

The chance they took seemed ill advised, as a post-season sleet storm arrived. However, Harold kept losses to a minimum through skill, effort, and ingenuity. His ear could distinguish from all other sounds the bleat of a sheep giving birth. At the first sign of distress he followed the sound to its source, served as veterinarian as necessary, and kept ewe and lamb together until each accepted the other. When he found a lamb separated from its mother he scrubbed it dry with rags, force-fed it with condensed milk, and bound it to any ewe that had lost her own lamb, until the relationship between orphan and foster mother had cemented.

We lambed out at a hundred percent and held the band at pasture until the lambs were frisky enough for docking, castrating, dipping, and trailing to the summer range. Harold described the next procedure.

"Albert's got the best layout. We'll bring the four bands together at his spread for the next step. Sheep don't need tails so we cut 'em off. We call it dockin'. The weight that goes into the tail goes into the lamb, so we gain a few pounds by the time we send the weathers to market. We don't need bucks. We've got two dozen of the horny critters. That's all we need to service the herd. So we dock all the lambs and castrate all the bucks.

**(Author's note: Sensitive readers may wish to skip the next four paragraphs. It's raw stuff. I have recorded it because sometimes life was, and is, raw.)**

"We push the lambs, one at a time, along a chute. If a ewe lamb comes through, we pass it along to dockin' and dippin'. If a buck comes through, one guy upside-downs and holds him, another cuts a slit in his bag, another de-nuts him, another whacks off his tail and pushes him through the dippin' tank to kill off the ticks.

"The lowest man on the totem pole always gets the short end of the stick. You're low man, so you'll be expected to de-nut. You can use your fingers or your teeth. Sheep nuts are slippery little devils. If I was you I'd use my teeth. Bury your head down there and nip off the nuts one after another. Pretty soon it's just routine. Back off timid and it's a hell of a job".

I followed Harold's advice and dived in head first. Ugh! I thought that being covered with sheep shit while tromping wool was a nasty experience. It <u>was</u> nasty. It was <u>not</u> nasty nasty as this was, moving my mouth amidst blood and excreta in search of testicles that slithered to escape my bite.

Having learned to muckle into nasty assignments, however, I survived the ordeal. With the taste of blood still in my mouth and the stale odor of urine still in my nostrils, I approached Uncle Henry for my pay.

"My God, Cy," he said. "there must be a misunderstanding. Your dad is behind on his share of the herd bill and I thought you were working to help pay it off."

"Hmmm . . . I guess that's right, Henry," I said, a young man disheartened, but wiser in the ways of the world.

*    *    *    *

During my stint as unpaid assistant to a sheepherder, Dave continued alone in his search for work. Upon my return we joined forces and found occasional jobs that allowed us to eat at a subsistence level. We learned that eating habits are regulated by the seasons: what people eat depends upon what they like, what is available, and what they can afford. We ate what we could afford, which wasn't much.

Back home, late at night, we listened to the radio. Our crystal set, with the bedspring as antenna, brought to our Baldwin headphones our favorite program: KFI, San Francisco, featuring Frances Langford singing at the St. Frances Hotel. When that program was followed by a dismal report on life in the city, we shifted to KOA, Denver, then to KHJ, Los Angeles, or KSL, Salt Lake. Beamed from every station, life was described in the raw. One night Dave said, "Cy, we're not needed at home. This damn depression can't be that bad everywhere. We might as well take the plunge. Let's hit the road."

"That's okay by me. I'm sure you won't pull a 'Dean Conover' trick and get married before we go?"

"What do you mean?"

74

"I never told you before, but here's the story. When I was fresh out of high school Dean and I planned to ride his motorcycle to Alaska and seek our fortunes. While I was getting my gear together, he went to Eureka to bid farewell to one of his buddies. He took a shine to one of the sisters and started thinking about how cold it is in Alaska. After a bit he suggested that they get married. She agreed and they got married.

"When Dean returned to Salt Lake, he passed it off like this, 'That's no problem. I'll just add a sidecar to the motorcycle, so there's room for three.' There might have been room for three, but I didn't want to be the third one in a triangle.

"Speaking of a third one, maybe Jim Myers would like to go along. He'd add some spice to life. I'll check him out."

Jim was a free spirit, ready to go. Dave and I were free spirits, too, but we knew that life ahead would be no lark. We didn't want to go, but we felt there was no alternative.

Dave and I weren't sure how best to disclose our plans to Mother, but knowing her regard for honest talk we chose to break the news straight out. "Mom," Dave said, "we've tried everything we could think of to find work around here. We can't seem to make a go of it, so we plan to strike out for greener pastures. We'll find something somewhere. We don't know where, but every few days we'll drop you a postcard so you'll know where we are, and that we're all right."

After hesitating for a time to get her emotions under control, she said, "I've been half expecting this. I can understand your frustrations. Everything seems uncertain. I won't worry about you. Our worst misfortunes are those that never happen."

Mother knew frustration, too. She smiled through developing tears and bade us good luck. She knew her boys and trusted their judgment.

# PART 2

# HOBOES

# Chapter 7

# Riding the Rails

On the Fourth of July, 1933, brother Dave, buddy Jim, and I headed for the Salt Lake railroad yards. "What are your plans, Dave?" Jim asked.

"We'll board the first freight train outa the yard," Dave said. "It doesn't matter where it's headed, we'll celebrate Independence Day by being independent. We'll not be tramps, beggars, vagabonds, or carefree ne'er-do-wells. We'll ride the rails from crop to seasonal crop and give a full day's work for a fair day's pay. We'll make it. Somehow, somewhere, we'll make it. Okay, fellows?"

On the western fringe of Salt Lake City spread the classification yards of the Union Pacific Railroad. The area was surrounded by an eight-foot fence posted with no-trespass signs to dissuade the timid, and crowned with a barbed wire parapet to restrain the bold.

We moseyed along the city street that bordered the fence, casting furtive glances at the shifter, the yard locomotive, as it switched cars from one track to another. We were neither timid nor bold, merely apprehensive as we discussed how we could best climb aboard the freight train being assembled in the yards beyond that fence. We ambled along, dawdled at the street corner, and ambled some more at a leisurely pace to avert the attention of the switching crew and the bull.

Our plans evolved slowly as we bandied suggestions, then rapidly as ideas spawned more ideas. Dave summarized our plan: "The fence ends at the yard limit. That's only a mile or so. We'll move along and at the highball signal we'll run toward the caboose. The train crew will be occupied with routine duties. If the bull doesn't see us, there'll be no problem. If he does see us, what can he do if our timing is right? He has to pile off before the train picks up too much speed. When he piles off, we pile on. Timing is the thing."

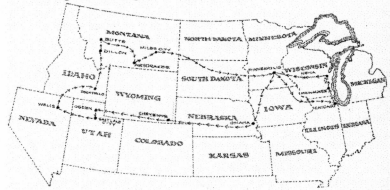

**Route of the hobo journey from Salt Lake City and return**

We strode toward the northern yard limit. Excellent timing, we thought, as the lead engine, with bell ringing, chugged through the highway intersection that marked the limit of the freight yard. It tooted the highball signal and picked up speed.

We managed to board a gondola. It was loaded with ties stacked cosswise. They were snugged firmly against the rear of the car, leaving a three-foot gap at the front where we were comfortable and hidden from view. Occasionally we stood up to chart our course across the hot desert countryside.

For several miles our course was due north, then it veered in a wide sweep to the west. Jim was first to comment. "I thought we were headed toward Boise. Now it looks like San Francisco, here we come."

"What difference does it make?"

As he glanced at his light suede jacket, Jim replied, "It's probably warmer in the fields of Idaho than in the fog of San Francisco."

The train rumbled mile after mile with a gentle rhythm, the wheels making staccato clickity-click-click sounds as they passed over the joints where the rails met end to end. Then a new sound appeared, a deep crunch-crunch as the coupling of our gondola rammed into the boxcar ahead, the coupling of the boxcar following rammed into our gondola, and each following car slammed into the one ahead.

"The engineer has pulled back on the throttle," Dave said. We're coming to a stop, and he's letting her coast."

Sure enough, the rhythm was broken. We could sense the crunch-crunch of cars alternately pushing and pulling. One long toot from the engine and we ground to a stop.

We've hit either a station or a siding," Dave said. "I'd judge from this God-forsaken country it's a siding and we'll lay over till a passenger train highballs through. Cy, why don't you take a look?"

"Yep, we're on a siding, with not a living thing in sight." It was quiet, oppressively quiet. Jim started to hum. He added a word here and there. His rich tenor began tentatively to sing, then rose loud and clear to the melancholy strain

> *Once I built a railroad; made it run.*
> *Made it race against time.*
> *Once I built a railroad; now it's done.*
> *Brother, can you spare a dime?*
> *Once I built a tower; to the sun.*
> *Brick and rivet and lime.*
> *Once I built a tower; now it's done.*
> *Brother, can you spare a dime?*
> *Once in khaki suits, gee we ..*

A brusque command, "get the hell outa there!" brought us back to reality as the brakeman peered over the side of the gondola. "You'd get killed dead in that trap hole if the train stopped quick and the ties slammed ahead. Then wouldn't my ass be in a sling! Go find an empty boxcar. You've got maybe twenty minutes. Damn fool kids," he muttered, as he disappeared over the side.

"Damn fools," Dave agreed. "I thought brakies had a mean streak, but that one is all right. Let's find an empty."

Half a dozen cars back we found a boxcar with the door ajar. Jim gave Dave and me a leg up, then climbed aboard. Several men were lounging in one end of the car. We inched in the other direction to be with our backs to the wall. The farther we moved the more putrid the odor. We slithered back to the door and made a hasty exit.

A few cars farther along another door was ajar. We climbed aboard and found a single occupant in one end. I broke the tension: "Do you mind if we join you?"

"No, I don't mind, but she's got a flat wheel and rides rougher'n hell."

"Then why do you ride her?"

"Cause I like my own company."

"Hmmm."

The strained silence was broken by the approach of another train, a freight with two engines. As we watched it pass, the older man joined us. In better light, pockmarks shown on his swarthy face. His rough countenance and rugged build made us wary. However, he gave us no cause for concern. Besides, there was only one of him and three of us. To nobody in particular, I said, "Did you notice, there wasn't an empty car on that train? The flatcars and gondolas were loaded, and all the boxcar doors were sealed."

"You fellers must be new to the road, Whitey," our host volunteered. "Everybody knows that freights run mostly loaded headed east and empty headed west. I'll tell you something. When you find a car that's occupied you don't say 'Do ya mind if we join ya?' You say, 'Is this one full?' Even if there's only one guy inside and he says yes, you know he wants to be alone, and you respect his privacy."

"Thanks for the advice, mister, Dave said. "We're green, but we learn quick. We'd like to learn the ropes without making too many mistakes along the way."

"Don't call me mister, Shorty. Call me Blackie. And you better get used to Shorty, cause that's what you'll be called, no matter what road you ride. Your buddies'll be called Whitey and Slim cause that's what they be. If you don't know what to call a man, call him Mac. The sooner you learn the code of the road, the better off you'll be."

Dave bristled when he was called Shorty. To be short was a burden he had borne gracefully on the surface, but inside he was deeply sensitive that he hadn't been granted a few more inches of height. I could sense his inward turmoil, and felt relieved when Jim, newly christened Slim, joined in the banter.

"Blackie," he said, "I'm like Dave and I'm sure Whitey, too. We sppreciate your advice and would like some more pointers on the code of the road. It's no good to learn everything the hard way, but how do you know what's right when you've never done it before?"

Blackie went on. "The jungle provides a good grapevine and a good place to learn the ropes. Keep it that way. You'll find there's a hobo jungle near the yards of all the division stops on the railroad. There's so damn many transients nowadays the towns find it better to keep 'em apart where there's water and campfire sites than to have 'em all over town. The cops won't bother ya if you don't make a problem for 'em.

"In general I'd say: Always leave the jungle better than ya find it. Don't come near some other guy's campfire unless you've got an invite. If ya make coffee, never throw out the grounds. The next feller might not have none. Don't give false tips about good handouts and missions, or friendly bulls and boodle towns. Most important, like I say, the jungle provides a good grapevine. Keep it thataway."

"Shorty and I were raised in a mining camp, Blackie," I said. "We thought we'd hit Butte for a job of work, but maybe we'd better not. Say, what are divisions?"

"Divisions are them towns along a railroad that have maintenance facilities. They're spaced a few hundred miles apart to jibe with the normal hitch of the train crew. They usually have a jungle handy to the yards. If ya wanta make good time you can freshen up during the layover and catch the same train out. But after six or eight hours on a freight you're ready for a snooze."

"Blackie, where's the best place to find work? When we left Salt Lake it didn't seem to matter where we headed. Maybe you can tell us the best direction to take."

"Follow the kinda harvest that depends on transient labor. You're too late for the southern crops. California's run over with Mexicans, Chinee, and Okies. Besides, that's mostly stoop work. You're too early for pickin' spuds in Idaho or apples in Washington. You might get a month in the hay, then hit the wheat crop in the Dakotas.

"We'll make Wells, Nevada sometime tonight. There's a branch line from Wells to Pocatello where you hit the main line to Montana. Now let's get a little shut-eye. Lucky this was a grain car lined with heavy paper. Tear some of it off the walls. You'll find that Hoover blankets are pretty good to keep the cold out."

We tore large pieces of heavy brown paper off the walls, as he suggested, and curled up in our Hoover blankets for sleep made fitful by gnawing hunger.

We were lucky, I thought, to have run into Blackie on our first day on the road. He's not a bad guy, and I guess we can't hold it against him for having had smallpox when he was a kid. It's strange how things work out. If Jim hadn't started to sing, the brakeman wouldn't have known we were in that death trap. We might be dead, but we're not. Maybe we'll be lucky all the way. This car sure rides rougher'n, hell, as Blackie said. It could be worse, but life could be better, too, like listening to Frances Langford sing over radio station KFI as we used to, or seeing her in person at the St. Francis Hotel. Or like eating a steak, a sandwich, or even a raw potato. Hmmm, I wonder if Dave and Jim are as hungry as I am. They wouldn't admit it if they were. Neither would I, except to myself. I wonder what they're thinking about.

One long whistle, and I knew what Dave was thinking about. "Get up, fellows, we must be approaching Wells. We oughta pile off soon as we hit the yards. We don't want to get tangled up with the bull."

"Relax, Shorty," Blackie said. "Wells is a good town and, besides, we're some time yet getting into the yards. Like I say, they won't cause trouble if you don't ask for it. Just mind your own business and keep outa the way. Don't cross 'em and they'll save their meanness for guys that do. One thing you outa do is learn the railroad signals, both the lantern signals and the whistles. It'll help your peace of mind."

"Much obliged, Blackie. We appreciate your advice."

Dawn was breaking as we slowed, approaching Wells. The air was chilly. Jim rubbed his hands together briskly, then danced a little jig. He tore a hole in one of his Hoover blankets and stuck his head through it. "This is a pretty good poncho," he said, as he pulled it tightly around him. "I think I'll take it with me. A blanket and a coat, all in one light bundle."

Blackie was headed for California. We said "so long, and thanks again," then jumped to the ground and scampered across the yards to the main street of Wells, Nevada.

Wells was laid out on a flat stretch of the Salt Lake to San Francisco highway. The main street cut a wade swath at right angles to that road. On one side spread the town, on the other, the railroad yards. Clouds of alkali dust rose as we walked. The endless expanse of silvery gray-green sagebrush blended into the distant dun-colored mountains.

Nature had endowed this place so sparingly that we felt like moving rapidly beyond. Yet the raw reach of this primitive country, the stillness, and the rugged wilderness all combined to make it a special place, and of this moment a special occasion. The smell of sagebrush in the early morning was crisp. The rising sun felt good. It warmed the body, renewed the soul, and cast our thoughts on breakfast.

As we walked the length of the main street, and back, the town came alive. The two places of greatest interest, the diner and the bakery, were both open.

"Let's try the diner," Jim suggested. "It smells pretty good to me. Maybe we can get breakfast and wash dishes to pay for it."

"It won't work." Dave said. "Maybe one of us could make it, but not all three. Now here's the best deal. We've got ten cents and a counterfeit two-bit piece. Cy, you can probably pull it off. Go in the bakery and look your hungriest. Do the best you can for ten cents worth, and try to pass the bogus quarter. If that bounces, give up the dime, and we've still got the two-bit piece as backup."

We agreed with Dave's logic, and struck out for the bakery. The aroma that greeted us was heaven itself.

"Okay," I said, "let's all stand around the window so when I go in he can see how hungry we are, and know that I'm bargaining for three of us and not just one."

I went in and looked over the bakery goods long enough to display my hunger, but not so long as to annoy the clerk. "What does it cost for a loaf of day-old bread?"

Regular price is four cents a loaf for day-old punk. I can give you a twenty-ounce loaf."

"That's good. I'll take a loaf and six cents worth of day-old cakes or cookies, the kind that's most nourishment for the money."

The waiter stuffed a loaf of bread and some cookies in a paper bag, looked at me, added a few more cookies, and placed the bag on the counter. I slid the two-bit piece to him. He threw in on the shelf of the cash register, automatically punched ten cents, then with a pained expression flipped the coin between his thumb and forefinger into the air so it landed on the counter. It landed with a thud. He slid it toward me and retrieved the bag of goodies.

"That's bogus!"

"My God, I didn't know. Here, I've got a dime. Try that."

He glanced at it and passed me the merchandise. During the course of the transaction another customer had entered the bakery. I thought it strange that when the quarter was exposed as counterfeit he made a hasty exit. As I left the store he was waiting for me.

"Hey, Mac," he said, "I'll give you a dime for that two-bit piece. I think I can pass it."

"Just a minute," I said, and conferred with my buddies.

"It's a deal."

We exchanged coins and went our separate ways.

"Come on, Dave, stretch your legs," Jim kidded, as we strode toward the far end of the yards to enjoy breakfast and await train departure.

"Let's eat the bread first," Dave suggested, "and have the sweets for dessert. We'd better have most of our goodies for supper tonight. That is, unless something better shows up in the meantime."

With his pocket knife Dave made two lines on the loaf of bread. He cocked his head back to survey the fairness of the three-way division.

"Damn it," Jim growled, "I can stand the ecstasy of this agony just so long. Don't mind me, Dave, that's a fancy phrase I learned in Miss. Connelly's English class. Seriously, never did a loaf of stale bread look so good. Let's get on with the job."

With a chuckle Dave got on with the job. With bread in hand and a wink to me, he feigned indifference to hunger and started a casual conversation. Jim pinched out a morsel of the soft central portion to savor it.

"The hell with you guys!" he exploded. I'm going to eat."

We all laughed at our little joke, ate the bread and a couple of cookies each, and stretched out for a good rest while waiting for the train. We were content. Jim displayed his pleasure with a bit of humming, then a few scattered words, and finally with the rendition of one of his favorite songs.

*Just around the corner*
*There's a rainbow in the sky.*
*So let's have another cup of coffee,*
*And let's have another piece of pie.*
*You know that trouble's just a bubble,*
*And the clouds will soon go by.*
*So let's have another cup of coffee,*
*And let's have another piece of pie.*

Two long whistle blasts from the locomotive interrupted Jim's refrain. We scurried toward the approaching train and managed, while it was still moving slowly through the yards, to board an empty boxcar. Jim, tall and agile, clambered in first with a combination hand-grab, jump, and dive, then helped Dave and me scramble aboard.

"Thanks for the help, Jim," Dave said. "Good thing we screwed up our courage to board her in the yards. If she'd been going at a much faster clip I'd never have made it."

The train rumbled northward through a wide plain between two mountain ranges. It gained elevation slowly at first, then rapidly as the engines labored to gain speed up the grade. The vast sprawl of monotonous landscape gradually changed as we approached the brown shoulders of the mountains. On the upper reaches of this hot and arid land, sagebrush, undisputed master of the vast domain, shared its realm with junipers and pinon pines.

This is mustang country, I reflected, where the measure of triumph is survival, and the stallion reigns supreme. This is Roy Lazzenbee country, where he learned the skills he shared with me as a boyhood helper on his ranch. Roy was my idol. I recalled those happy days with him when I was a thirteen-year-old lover of horses, guns, and automobiles.

My reverie ended abruptly as Dave rose to investigate a strange sound that interrupted the rhythmic clickity-click of our boxcar. During the heat of the day we had partially closed the doors to shut out the bright sunshine, blocking them slightly ajar to keep them from slamming shut. We didn't relish the prospect of being locked in a boxcar that might be shunted for days to an idle siding.

Dave opened one door and called Jim and me to look. "My God, fellows, we've run into a swarm of traveling locusts, millions of 'em. They're so greasy that when we run over 'em the train loses traction. That funny sound we hear is the engineer releasing sand to the rails to keep us moving."

We kept moving for several hundred yards, slowly, until the train passed over the swarm of locusts, then gradually resumed speed. I thought of the sea gulls that had saved Brigham Young and his followers from famine when their first crops were threatened by these voracious pests. What a feast this swarm would have made for those sea gulls!

Our spirits rose as the train moved from the desolation of the desert into the lush farming area of the Snake River Plain of Idaho. It made brief stops at Twin Falls, Burley, Rupert, Minidoka, then a major layover at Pocatello, a division junction. The main line from Pocatello continued east to Omaha. A branch line carried traffic north to Montana.

At Pocatello we learned that a northbound freight would leave for Montana in the morning and stop briefly at Blackfoot. We decided to hitch a ride to Blackfoot and try our luck in that town. If nothing showed up we would catch the train to Montana from there. We found our way to the road and caught a ride with a farmer. The truck he was driving eventually slowed to a stop.

# Chapter 8

## Bean Dinner Fantasy

"I'm takin' the next turn left," the farmer said. "I stopped to show where you might scare up a feed. There's a well back of that old farmhouse. Mrs. Jensen, up the road, had a crew come in and thresh out the beans. The rig rejects both the little ones and the big ones. If you sift around in the chaff you'll find enough little ones to make a full pot. Don't mix in the big ones. It'll take too long to cook 'em."

"Thank you for the ride, sir, and for your advice."

We headed for the old farmhouse. The screen door to the back porch was open, so we went inside. Half a dozen photographs, tied with a faded ribbon, were lying face-up in an old baby buggy. Hairline cracks flawed their yellowed surfaces. One of the pictures was an enlargement of a family group. This farmhouse, trim and newly painted, was in the background. Proud parents and three smiling children were in the foreground.

A sense of sadness crept upon us. Perhaps the departed owners may return in better times and reclaim these mementos of a happier day. We returned the pictures, face side down, to the buggy.

At the other end of the porch were articles that had been discarded but never quite thrown out. These abandoned things, we rationalized, were fair prey in our time of need.

"Look, here's a ten-pound lard bucket that oughta be good for cookin' the beans," Jim said, "and some old spoons to boot. We can use these cans to collect the beans and then use 'em as bowls when we eat. Beans to eat, a bowl to eat out of, and a spoon to eat with. What more could a fellow ask for?"

"I could ask for a good bath," Dave replied. "I'm going to take one if this old washtub doesn't leak. We'll make a fire, heat the bath water, and then cook the beans. They'll take a lot of cookin', so we'd better do that first. In the meantime we can take a bath."

As the farmer had said, the pickings were good. We collected a pail of undersize beans and returned to the wood pile. We made a fire, pumped water from the well, and while it was heating for the bath sat down to contemplate.

"Pork goes with beans like ham goes with eggs," I said. "We oughta have some pork. Now I wonder. If I walk up the road and get acquainted with Mrs. Jensen in just the right way, maybe I can scare up a little without having to ask for it. I think I'll give it a try."

That I did. "Hello, Mrs. Jensen. My name is Cy and I know yours. The man who gave us a ride told us that Mrs. Jensen is a nice lady and probably wouldn't mind if we picked some beans out of her stack of chaff. My two buddies and I have sorted out some beans and made a fire down by that old farmhouse. But we don't know how to cook beans. I thought maybe you could tell us how to go about it."

"That was nice of him," she said. Hmmm . . . I wonder who it was. Well, there's no secret about cookin' beans. First you soak 'em overnight. Then you add some chunks of pork and cook 'em in a pressure cooker till they're tender. Then you add molasses or brown sugar, and shift 'em to the oven till you're ready to eat."

"Hmmm, there's more to cookin' beans than I realized. That is, if you're going to do it right. I'm wondering what's the next best way. That is, if you're too hungry to wait for 'em to soak, or if you don't have a pressure cooker, an oven, or even any pork? What if you have a lard bucket to cook 'em in, and an open fire to cook 'em on?"

"You don't have to soak 'em. That just speeds things up. But you do need a pressure cooker or they'll never cook. I'll tell you what to do. Use a cover on your lard bucket and weight it down with a rock. When pressure builds up too high the lid will lift. When the steam escapes it will settle back down."

"Good idea, ma'am. I wouldn't have thought of it. That takes care of one problem. If we don't have an oven we won't

92

have baked beans.  We'll have stewed beans instead. That'll solve that problem. Thank you very much, ma'am. I'll be getting along. If a fellow is hungry enough, stewed beans will taste like pork pie and dumplings."

"That reminds me. I can spare a little pork. Beans taste pretty bland without seasoning. Come in a minute and I'll dig around."

I followed her into the house. Two boys in their early teens were playing checkers. Mrs. Jensen went down the cellar and returned with a slab of pork. She cut off a chunk and placed it in a paper bag, along with some salt and a smidgen of pepper

"There," she said, as she followed me outside and gently touched my shoulder. "That'll help. Good luck to you."

"Thank you, Mrs. Jensen. Those are fine looking boys you have. I don't mean to be personal, ma'am, but they sure could use a haircut.  One of my buddies is a pretty fair barber. He could cut their hair if you have a pair of scissors. Shall I send him up?"

"They are good boys," she beamed. "Their hair is pretty shaggy.  Please do ask him to come. I have some scissors and also some clippers their father used to use on them."

"I'll tell you what, ma'am," I said. "We're pretty crummy. Soon as Dave takes a bath in an old washtub we found he'll be right along."

"A bath? Just a minute," she said. "Here's a bar of soap. I make it myself and have plenty. It's harsh and mostly good for laundry, but it's better than nothin. And here's an old pie plate. It's beat up around the edges but still flat in the middle. It'll make a good lid for your lard bucket."

I added the soap and pie plate to my other loot, thanked her again, and returned to the farmhouse to report my good fortune.

I helped Dave carry the tub of hot water to the porch. He stripped and took a long and noisy bath. Between contented grunts of pleasure he bellowed forth in a rusty voice a few lines from his favorite song.

What a glorious feeling is brought forth, I thought, by a tub of hot water and a bar of homemade soap.

Dave dressed and left to cut the Jensen boys' hair. Jim took his turn at the tub. I tended the beans. When Jim finished I took a bath and he tended the beans. We were both tending the beans when Dave returned, all smiles.

"That's a lovely lady," he said. "When I got through cutting the boys' hair she said, 'Those beans will taste a lot better with molasses in 'em. I put some in a can for you. And you oughta have some bread to go with 'em. Here's part of a loaf I can spare.' Isn't that something?"

Jim added wood to the fire and sampled the beans. "They've swelled some, but they're still too hard to eat," he said. Now if I took a walk up the road I wonder if that nice lady would find something we could nibble on. No, that's not a good idea."

"You're right, Jim, it's not," Dave said "but the idea is a good one. Matter of fact, I've been thinking on it myself and have got it all figured out. It'll take time but that's what we want to use up. Since I've got the details in mind I'll be the boss. Okay?

"Now here's the deal. We'll have a three-course dinner. Jim, you do the first course. Make a bed of embers out of the fire. Use the lid of the lard bucket for a frying pan. Fish six pieces of pork out of the beans. Cook 'em slowly till they're nice crisp cracklings. We'll eat them first.

"Cy, you fix the next course. To one part fat that's left over from Jim's cooking, add two parts of molasses. Blend it into a syrupy dip. Toast six slices of bread to a golden brown, then break 'em into bits. That'll be our crackers to go with the dip. Use one of the old screens from the porch as a toaster. Don't worry about bugs. The fire will kill 'em.

"As for the main course, the beans will be flavored with the pork and what's left of the molasses. A Hoover blanket spread over the chopping block will make a nice table. We'll squat around it and munch crackers and dip. If we eat slow and deliberate, it'll keep us occupied till the main course is ready. Let's get to work."

Jim was in the final stage of rendering the pork, turning the cracklings over and over. "Okay boss," he said, "The aperitifs are ready. Let's eat."

As we nibbled the first course, slow and deliberate as Dave had specified, we prepared and served the second course. We relished every morsel in studied leisure. This dalliance was a self-imposed restraint. We lingered for the avowed purpose of giving time to cook the beans. The deeper motive was to prolong this festive occasion, this moment of intimate companionship.

"Men," Dave said, "the odor is fetching, the flavor sublime, but the color is eggshell white. Maybe we should have added the molasses earlier. Let's call 'em beanos blanco and dig right in." We cut the remaining bread into three chunks, filled our bowls with beans, and ate with uninhibited gusto.

The warmth of the fire was pleasant in the developing chill of evening. Sparkling embers added syncopation to the singing rhythm of distant locusts. Rustling of sparse leaves on the gnarled shade trees waxed and waned, always subdued, as whiffs of wind changed direction. The droning sound of an automobile -- its approach, its passing, its distinctive whine in moving on -- annoyed our sensitivities. Why can't that car be somewhere else and allow us the privacy of our thoughts? Why here?

The car was quickly gone. We returned to the bean pot for second and third helpings. After a bit of bantering we retired to the porch and snuggled under Hoover blankets for a good night's sleep.

For me, sleep was a long time coming. Too many thoughts contended for attention. Have I, in two days on the road, absorbed the philosophy of vagabonds: Enjoy today for we know not what tomorrow brings. Or have my buddies and I been living a fantasy? What is real? What is fancied? I pondered long into the night.

In that hazy realm between sleep and thought, I finally faced reality. Our happy interlude is over. Our next meal will not be a whimsical feast; it will be a bucket of cold beans. When the beans are gone, we'll have just one thin dime. We better be prepared to face it. I went to sleep.

Jim and I roused the next morning to find that Dave had already made a fire and warmed the beans. We had a hearty breakfast of beans, doused the fire, and found our way to the railroad yard. The freight train, as scheduled, made a brief stop at Blackfoot. We found an empty and hopped aboard.

# Chapter 9

# Skill is What You Make It

*"I returned, and saw under the sun, that the race is not to the swift, nor the battle to the strong, neither yet bread to the wise, nor yet riches to men of understanding, nor yet favor to men of skill; but time and chance happeneth to them all."*

Ecclesiastes 9:11-12

One long compelling blast of the locomotive whistle signalled our approach to Dillon, Montana. As the train came to a stop in the yards, Dave peered out to get his bearings and see if the coast was clear. Apparently satisfied, he beckoned Jim and me to follow. He seated himself at the doorway with legs outstretched as far as he could reach, then slid to the ground. Jim and I followed. We gathered our gear and scooted across the yards in the direction of town.

"Look at the boxcars on that siding," I said. "Judging from the rust on the rails they've been there a long time. Let's check 'em out. If one looks good we'll have a place to stay and a meeting place if we get separated."

The door of the first car we checked slid easily on its track. Apparently while standing idle this boxcar had sheltered many hoboes in need of a bunk. Piles of crumpled paper confirmed that assessment. The odor was stale but not foul. Former occupants had observed the rules of the road.

"That was a good idea, Cy." Jim said. "Let's call this our home away from home and start with a feed of beanos mucho frio. Then we can cache the bean bucket in the weeds and case the town. I'll put my pencil with the beans so if we get separated we can write notes to each other on the inside of the door."

Dillon was a town of contradictions. To the hordes of transient humanity that moved aimlessly about the country, Dillon was a mere wait-station, a stop on an endless journey. To farmers and ranchers seeking transient laborers for harvesting their seasonal crops, it was a convenient hiring center. To us and others seeking work where willing muscle was in demand, it was a likely watering trough, an oasis in otherwise desolate setting. We found it to our liking.

We inquired of a man pumping gas at a filling station, "Excuse us, please. Maybe you can tell us where we'd be most likely to run into somebody looking for help. Where do the ranchers go when they want to hire men?"

The attendant appeared pleased to share his views with us. "We don't have no hiring hall here. Now to think of it, that's something the Grange could damn well do, especially during the busy season. If a rancher wants to hire some help he'll sometimes go down to the depot when a freight's due in. He might find a good man from last year coming through for another turn. If not, he'll have a chance to look over the hoboes as they crawl off the freight, and take his pick. But There's no train due for a while. Then he might go down to Pete's Pool Hall and lounge around till he spies somebody that might work out good. But there again you've got a problem. They don't come to town till after supper. You've got quite a wait. If it was me I'd just relax and I can relax one place as good as the other. So I'd mosey back and forth between Pete's place and the depot till something turns up. The hell of it is, the season is well along and most of the crews are filled up. You won't have much chance if you hang together."

We thanked the man for his advice, took a drink of water, and laid our plans: We'll split up. Dave will take the depot. Jim and I will take the pool hall. We'll keep each other informed of our activities by writing notes on the boxcar door, as Jim suggested. If for any reason we can't do that, we'll write post cards to the others in care of general delivery.

Dave headed for the depot. Jim and I moseyed down to the pool hall. We had no problem finding it. Signs in the windows announced in bold black letters, PETE'S BILLIARD PARLOR. Inside were four regulation pool tables, two snooker tables, and, in the back of the room, four card tables arranged with four chairs each.

In one of the front corners of the room the proprietor sat on a high stool at a counter that displayed tobacco goods and several kinds of candy bars. A cigar box served as depository for the cash receipts. A sign on the wall stated, Pool -- 10 Cents a Round. The walls were lined with chairs. Above them were racks of billiard cues. Two of the pool tables were in use as was one of the card tables. Several onlookers were enjoying the pool games and two men were kibitzing the card game.

We approached the attendant. I said, "Excuse me, please, we're looking for work and have been told that sometimes ranchers and farmers come here looking for help. If you don't mind, we'll tarry a bit in hopes something might turn up."

"No, I don't mind. It's better to have a full house than an empty house, even if they're not all paying customers. Besides, fellows come here to find a job and when they make some money they sometimes come back and spend some of it.

After a bit of casual banter I sensed that we were getting along real well when he said, "You like to play pool?"

"I'd rather play pool than eat. That is, unless I'm powerful hungry. Matter of fact, I used to play for the house on occasion. Why?"

"That short, heavy fellow over there -- his name is Angus -- wants to roll a few rounds of pool. I'm all lamed up so I can't play him myself. If you're any good you can play him for the house. If he loses, he pays; if you lose, you don't. Just make sure you win two games out of three. Okay?

That was a fair proposition. I asked Angus if he'd like to roll a few. He said, Sure, Call Shot?

I said, Sure, and we selected our cues.

Angus lumbered around the pool table as though his every joint were rheumatic. Whatever his ailment, it hadn't affected his vocal chords. He talked incessantly.

I won the first game, he the second, I the third. Well into the fourth game, Dave burst in, all smiles, to announce that he had a job helping a farmer harvest peas. That was all he knew about it.

He would see us in a few days, maybe four or five, and away he went.

Angus and I continued playing pool. I won the fourth game. We started the fifth. "This should be his game," I reckoned, "I can let down a bit. He is a nice guy and a pretty good pool player. He deserves to win at least one time out of three." Two men entered the pool hall and came toward our table. Angus greeted them.

"Hello, John. Hello, Breck. Nice to see you both. What brings you to town this time of day?"

"Hi, Angus," John answered. "I came hoping Joe O'Toole would be on the freight this afternoon, but he wasn't. Now I'm stuck with hay rotting in the field and no stacker."

My ears perked up. "Excuse me John," I said. "My name is Cy. If you need a stacker, I'm a stacker. And if you need a spare hand, my buddy Jim will work like hell for you."

John looked us over carefully. Evidently he was accustomed to sizing up men. Although of medium size, with muscular arms covered with hair bleached by the sun, he was not a typical field worker. He was the boss. His sidekick stayed in the background. Angus broke the awkward strain. "John, if he can stack hay like he wields a cue stick, he'll make a good man for you."

That support did the trick. John said, "I need a stacker, and to get one maybe I can use a spare hand. I'll give you a whirl. We pay the going rate for a ten-hour day. Buck'n a quarter in the field, and a buck-fifty on the stack. That's with a bunk and good grub. Okay? We've got some errands to run, and will be back for you in half an hour or so. Let's go, Breck. So long, Angus." And he was gone.

As we continued our pool game, Angus volunteered some information. "John is a hell of a good foreman. He works year round at the Sullivan farm and practically runs the place. The old man is over the hill. The old lady would be, too, without Colleen's help. Now there's an Irish lass for you, a real shamrock. If I was a young feller again, wouldn't I be sniffing around that!

100

"It's a dairy farm they run. They put up some volunteer hay, wild hay that grows on the prairie, you know. But mostly they put up alfalfa. A cultivated crop is a lot more work, but they figure alfalfa is better for milk cows. They put it up with boats instead of bull rakes. Not many of 'em use boats around here. You work good and John will be all right. Don't make a pass at Colleen and the old man will be all right. Here comes John for you. Good luck."

Jim and I piled onto the back of John's Model-A pickup, arranged the spare tire, tools, and boxes of foodstuff to provide comfortable standing space, and took in the sights as we rode southward through town. We turned to the right as we reached the outskirts. John veered from side to side on the country road to miss protruding rocks and chuckholes.

In the background, hazy in the developing darkness, rose the Bitterroot Mountains. In black silhouette they appeared as a graph. "The peaks on that graph are the high points in one's life," I thought, "the valleys the low points. We're moving toward one of the peaks." My fantasy ceased abruptly as John took a sharp right turn and ground to a stop in the yard of the Sullivan farm.

"That's the homestead," John said, indicating one of the two farm houses. Nodding toward the other, he said, "That's where we bunk, and the connecting room is where we eat. Breakfast at six o'clock, and we start work at seven. I'll honk the horn at a quarter to six to rouse the crew. You can follow me."

Breck carried groceries from the pickup to the homestead. John showed us to a room on the second floor of the bunkhouse. It was furnished with two cots, two chairs, and a small table on which were stacked several Western Story magazines and a tattered deck of cards. Jim and I played a game, then flopped for a good night's sleep.

Three honks from the horn of John's pickup roused us the next morning. Having slept in our clothes, we needed only to put on our shoes to be ready for whatever the day might bring. Outside the cookhouse were some benches and a washtub. We splashed ourselves with water and lounged on the benches,

101

awaiting developments. John, Breck, and four other men, the balance of the crew, joined us, and we introduced ourselves all around.

An old man emerged from the homestead. He limped toward one end of the porch where a triangle was supported from the ceiling by a short rope. He swung a metallic rod round and round inside the triangle, announcing meal time.

John held us back. "Let's wait for the old man to be seated," he said. "He kinda likes it that way. He's a nice old gentleman, and it won't do us no hurt to cater to his whims."

After an appropriate delay, during which we bantered a bit on how best to display society manners, we entered the eating room. The old man was seated at one end of a long table. He rose slightly, peered at us through iron gray brows, struck his plate with his spoon, and said, "Welcome to the Sullivan table. Sit down and enjoy it."

John needn't have cautioned us to respect the old man's whims. The cut of this man's jaw, the bearing of his head, the look in his eyes, each alone would command respect. In combination they displayed authority befitting a king.

He wore faded overalls, which, although shrunken by repeated wanderings, were still too large for his withered frame. In each cheek was a deep furrow, a remnant of what in better days must have been an engaging laugh wrinkle. Across his face, from furrow to furrow, bristled a magnificent mustache, gray except on the fringe of the upper lip where it was tobacco-juice brown. This is not an old man, I thought, just a man wracked by years of debilitating illness. What a specimen he must have been in his prime!

My thoughts were diverted from the old man by the entrance of his daughter Colleen, carrying a tray of ham and eggs in one hand, pancakes in the other. Hmmm, I thought, if that man was a specimen in his prime, here is reincarnation at age seventeen, and female to boot. Raven hair accented her fair complexion. Sky-blue eyes reflected innocence. Yet in her quick contemplative glance around the table, a provocative glint showed through.

She poured each of us a cup of coffee and returned to the kitchen. Mr. Sullivan said "heave ho," and we heaved ho with firsts and seconds. Colleen returned to see if we "needed something more." We didn't. She refilled our coffee mugs. She was solicitous of Jim's needs, I thought, extra solicitous. That's the way it always is. He doesn't go for the girls but the girls sure go for him.

My thoughts were interrupted by John. "It rained last night so we'll have to change our schedule. We'll give the sun a coupla hours to dry things off, then get to work. We'll cut the back field, and rake and cock the front field. If we don't get more rain, we'll stack tomorrow. I'll see you at the barn about nine o'clock and we'll get started."

John and Breck left to tend the livestock. Jim and I chatted idly with the rest of the crew. A little before nine o'clock we walked down to the barn and got our assignments for the day. John pointed out the areas where alfalfa was to be cut, where it had been cut, was now to be raked, and where it had been raked into windrows and was now to be cocked. He assigned two men to rakes, two men to mowing machines, and Jim and me to cocking hay. The other men harnessed their teams and hitched up as instructed. Jim and I turned to with pitchforks.

We walked to the far end of the field. Grasshoppers, yellowish green with speckles of black, jumped all about us. The windrows were uniformly spaced about twenty feet apart. A good crop of hay, I thought, and the guy on the rake knew what he was doing. My buddy Jim didn't know what he was doing, nor even what he was supposed to do. City wise but unskilled in the ways of manual work, he was miscast as a field hand, and we both knew it.

"Here's the idea, Jim," I said. "When we haul this hay to the barn, we want it to be easy to handle. When we're loading in the field we want to pitch as much hay onto the rack as we can for every stop. So we make cocks out of rows and we space them uniformly so two guys can pitch at the same time, one from each side of the hay rack. We want each cock of hay to be as big as a man can muckle but not too big. The cocks will be about twenty-five feet apart along the windrows. We'll just guess what twenty-five feet is, and work toward the middle.

"Notice that when the hay is mowed, the stems are all in one direction. It's a good idea to criss-cross them so the cocks will hang together when we pitch 'em on the rack. Now watch me to get the hang of it, then we'll each take a windrow and get some work done."

As a boy I had helped an uncle on his farm during busy seasons, and knew how to put up hay. Having got Jim started on the first windrow, I went to the second. I was half way back on the third as I met him laboring down the first. We stopped to chat.

"There is more to this than I realized." he said. "Maybe I'll pick it up by and by. Anyway, what's all the big hurry?"

"You don't want to get fired the first day do you, Jim?" I said "John knows what's a day's work for two men. You're new at this chore so I'd better move right along to make up the difference. Okay, Buddy?" We kept up the pace until the dinner bell rang. After a half-hour break, we started again. A little before quitting time we had cleared the field and were back at the barn. We asked John if there were something more he wanted us to do.

"No," he said, "that was a good day's work. Wash up and take it easy till supper."

For supper Colleen brought out an earthen crock of fresh garden peas and new potatoes steeped in cream sauce, pork chops, corn niblets, hot biscuits, and warm apple pie with cheese slices. She stood near the corner of the table, awaiting calls for seconds on pie. Colleen eyed Jim seductively. The old man eyed Colleen disapprovingly. In subtle awareness of this interplay, I eyed the old man apprehensively. Jim, oblivious of his central role in the silent drama, eyed his food.

John, unaware of the unfolding tension, relieved it abruptly. "After I check the stock I'm going to town to shoot a little pool. Anyone wants to, can ride in with me."

Breck left with John. The rest of us lounged in the yard. I manoeuvered Jim to our bunkhouse, hoping to get Satan behind us, and in the doing to preserve our jobs.

There was an additional man at the breakfast table next morning. John introduced his as Joe O'Toole, the regular stacker each year, whom John had brought back from town the previous night.

"Cy," John said, "Joe knows the ropes around here so I'll put him on the stack today and Jim on the derrick team. Bill can mow this morning and rake this afternoon. That'll leave four men to pitch on and haul from the field. You can pair up with Murray."

During breakfast I worried about Jim's forthcoming performance. Driving the derrick team was a menial job, normally assigned to one of the children in the farm family. Jim had no experience with horses. I was concerned that John might not have patience to see him through. I was relieved when he gave Jim a hand harnessing the derrick team.

Murray and I harnessed our team and hitched it to a hay rack. We selected pitch forks and took to the field. Murray was wiry, slight of build, and quick of movement. The way he handled the team, and his every action, displayed familiarity with the work at hand, and ability to perform it well. I was pleased to be paired with him, and determined to hold up my end.

"Murray," I said, "I've worked around farms from time to time, but I've never seen a hay rack like that one." The bed of the rig was a plank platform about six feet wide and ten feet long. It was mounted on four automobile wheels. The rear axle was rigid to the platform. The front axle was connected to a wagon tongue and joined to the platform through a central kingpin which allowed it to swivel. On top of the platform was spread a net, on either side of which were fastened ropes in the form of a sling.

"That kind of a hay rack is what we call a boat," Murray said. "It's nice and low for pitchin' on. We can load about fifteen hundred pounds pretty slick. That's a good jag for a

105

derrick team to handle. At the top of the barn we've got a pulley. One end of the cable running through it is hitched to the derrick team. On the other end we'll fasten both sides of a sling, with hay in the net between the two sides. One side of the sling will be coupled to a quick-disconnect. When the derrick team heists the load, we'll yank the disconnect. One side of the load will drop. The net will unroll, and the hay will fall out. It's a handy way to put up hay."

**Hay boat, a handy way to put up hay**

Murray drove the team to the near edge of the field and positioned the boat midway between two cocks. He pitched on one side and I on the other. He drove to the next stop. We pitched on and he drove to the next stop.

"Murray," I said, "I'm getting the hang of this now and I'll take every other turn driving to the next stop."

"That's good of you, Cy, but just leave things be. This is a good team. Pretty soon they'll get the idea what they're supposed to do and neither of us will have to drive. Cy, you did a helluva good job of cockin' this hay yesterday. When the cocks hang together, the pitchin' on goes quick."

"Thank you, Murray."

We fastened the sling together and drove to the barn. Joe O'Toole coupled the sling to the hook on one end of the cable. Murray moved alongside Jim.

"Jim," he said, "there's a little trick in this. I can tell you're kinda nervous. These old plugs have done this before. Just be quiet and hold a tight rein. Don't let 'em know you're green at the job and they'll be all right."

Murray took the reins in a firm grip, pursed his lips and made two loud kissing sounds. The team started forward slowly. It met resistance of the load, then lowered to the pull. Murray snapped the reins up and down on the horses' backs and cautioned them, "Go easy, boys, easy," as they moved forward and the sling neared the roof.

His sharp command, "Whoa!" stopped the team. Joe yanked the quick-disconnect of the sling. The load fell and the horses relaxed. Murray pulled back on the reins and urged the team to "Back up, boys, back up," until the hook was low enough for Joe to reach. He disconnected the sling and tossed it to me. Murray said, "Just do it like that, Jim, nice and firm, and you won't have no problem."

Murray took the reins of our team and drove toward the middle of the field. "Why don't we continue on the row that we started?" I asked.

"Well now," he replied, "it's like when you cocked the hay to make the pitchin' on good for the next feller. We want to make it good for Joe in the barn, so the loads don't come one right after the other. Give him time to spread one load before the next one is on 'em. We do that by keeping an eye on the other boat and going either as close or as far as we have to, to make the time lag between boats about even."

"Good idea, Murray," I said. This guy, I thought, is in there thinking all the time. He'd be a good fellow to tie to on the road.

The men on the other boat must have been as conscious of timing as Murray was. Soon we were delivering loads alternately at the barn in uniform sequence. Jim seemed to be controlling the derrick team with increasing self-confidence and pride in his performance.

We finished the day content with our progress. While awaiting the dinner bell I sensed Jim's absence and went to the barn to investigate. He was in the final stage of hanging harness to the pegs. We returned to the dining area for a bounteous meal.

Colleen displayed none of her usual sparkle. She was reserved and as petulant as a puppy caught in the middle of mischief. The old man kept his eyes glued to his plate, seemingly restrained from showing some strong emotion. The rest of us bantered halfheartedly, and after dessert strolled out to the yard. John motioned me aside.

"Cy," he said, I'll take you and Jim to town tonight."

"We don't have anything to go to town for, John."

"The old man told me to pay you off and take you to town."

"Pay us off? That means we're fired! My God, John, I've never been fired in my life and I can hold my own with any man alive."

"I'm sorry, Cy, but that's the way it is. The old man told me to pay you off. He gave me two an a quarter for each of you. Here it is."

"Two and a quarter each? I thought you paid a buck and a quarter a day. That's two-fifty each."

"No, that's two and a quarter. We only worked eight hours yesterday. That's the way the old man figures and he's the boss."

"Okay, John. I don't mind the short change but it hurts like hell to be fired. Tell Murray so long for me. I could pair up with him anywhere there's work to be done. Come on, Jim, lets go to town with John. We're fired."

John drove us to town. As we approached Pete's pool hall he broke the silence. "This is why it's tough to be a foreman."

"We understand, John. No hard feelings." We hopped out of the pickup and said so long.

*   *   *   *

Jim and I had a restless sleep at the rendezvous. Dave had left no message, and apparently was still harvesting peas. In the morning Jim was unusually quiet. I sensed that he was meditating on how best to broach his concern. I had not long to wait.

"Cy," he said, "I'm a burden on you and Dave. You'd do a hell of a lot better without me along. I'm not going to be a burden on anybody. I've decided to go back. Now I've got two and a quarter and I won't need that much to get back on. I'll tell you what. I'll buy us both a good breakfast, then strike out for home. No arguments please, buddy."

"Jim, don't blame yourself for us getting fired. The fact is, when Joe O'Toole showed up, John had more crew than he needed. Then Colleen took a shine to you and the old man didn't like it. You can't blame yourself for that. I wish she had taken a shine to me, but that's beside the point. We all have pluses and minuses. I'm a roughneck and my pluses are here on the road. You have something that I don't have and maybe your pluses are better served in the city. I just don't know."

"That's the way I figure it, Cy. That's why I'm going to head back to Salt Lake. Let's go have breakfast on me. I feel so flush with two and a quarter in my pocket I don't know how to act."

We had breakfast in the diner. Jim paid the bill and left a ten-cent tip. The waiter said, "Thanks a lot, Mac, I've got a wife and two kids, and every bit helps."

He had no way of knowing that that thin dime was a measure of our total assets a few days before. And yet, more than his words, the look of his eyes and the sincerity of his manner expressed appreciation of one poor soul for the kindness of another. We left the diner in quiet thought. This guy has a family. We have only ourselves to think about. With feigned nonchalance we moseyed across town to the main highway.

"Pay my respect to your mother and my regards to your sisters," I said. "Tell my mother we are doing fine and not to worry about us."

"I'll do it, Buddy."

"One more thing," I said, as I dug into my watch pocket. "Take this dime as a keepsake. Maybe fifty years from now, when we are old and gray, and maybe rich, we'll reminisce on

109

how we got this dime in trade for a counterfeit two-bit piece in Wells, Nevada."

"I'll do it, Buddy, so long."

"So long."

I was glad that Jim was not present later when John asked, "Where's your friend Jim, Cy?"

"I guess he got disillusioned, John, and left for home this morning."

"It's a good thing the old man couldn't get his hands on that damn fool kid this morning. He'd have wrung his neck. Do you know what he did? He didn't know how to take the harnesses off the team so he took 'em apart strap by strap. It took us an hour to put 'em back together again."

# Chapter 10

# In Search of Sanity

Having watched my friend Jim leave for home on a brave note, I grew melancholy. At a loss for something to do, I sauntered back to the depot. One large room served as both freight office and waiting room for passengers. The bulletin board displayed several notices and train schedules, all of which I studied at length. I mastered the contents but was none the wiser. It is surprising how much time a fellow can spend studying notices and train schedules; that is, if he has time on his hands and nothing better to do.

"Good morning," I said to the man in the office.

The station agent peered between the visor of his cap and the top of his spectacles.

"Morning," he said, and returned to his stack of papers.

"Nice day," I continued.

"Yup."

"Guess I'll take a little walk."

"Yup."

Sorry not to have something interesting to observe or wonder about, I strolled along the platform to the Railway Express office. The agent answered my pleasant greeting with a contemplative gaze, then a friendly response.

"Hello, lad. I've got a little sorting to do here. If you want to give me a hand, we'll have time for a cup of coffee before the next train comes in. Just put them cans of milk and the bread cartons out on the platform while I sort the rest of the outgoing freight. Then we'll fix up the inside to make room for the next load."

The Agent talked incessantly as we worked. Apparently he was as eager for an audience as I was for companionship. On

111

completing the job, he poured each of us a cup of coffee and asked, "Are you hungry, lad?"

"The coffee sounds good but I've had breakfast, thank you. Unless some work opens up pretty soon I'm going to have to get by on scanty fare and I might as well start getting used to it. There's not much activity around town, is there?"

"Dillon is a lively town in the winter when the college is in session. We have the State Normal School here. That's where teachers learn to teach."

"I wondered what that big cluster of buildings was. It seems a shame to have them idle all summer long."

"Well, they're not completely idle. As a matter of fact, we've got a summer session going on right now. I've got a daughter who is a teacher. She is taking a brush-up course in Domestic Art."

"Domestic Art," I said, sensing the agent's pride in his daughter, and wishing to give him an opening to elaborate. "That is cooking and nutrition and things like that, isn't it?"

"Yes, they get all kinds of training. They learn what's good for you and then how to cook it to make it taste good. That reminds me, lad, if you get real hungry and can't scare up a meal, you might go up to the Domestic Art building and offer yourself as a guinea pig to sample their wares. Don't go to the Domestic Science Department. That's where they learn to sew."

"Thanks for the suggestion, Mister, I'll do that. Now I'll mosey along and try to find some work. Thanks for the coffee."

The sun was now high in the sky, and the heat was oppressive. I walked across town to seek respite in the pool hall. Pete gave me a friendly greeting.

"It's nice to see you, Cy. What brings you to town today?"

"I'm sorry to say, Pete, that I'm out of work again. Things were going fine until old man Sullivam noticed what a shine his daughter was taking to my buddy Jim. The old fellow's taking no chances with that girl of his. He had John tie a can to our tail after supper last night."

That's too bad. Stick around and something might turn up. You can roll for the house while you're waiting."

Business was slow. As the afternoon dragged on, hunger pangs developed and I thought more and more about the Railway Express agent's suggestion. I left for the State Normal School and located the Department of Domestic Art.

"Miss," I said to the young lady, "don't you look lovely today. And here I am, the most receptive guinea pig that ever offered himself to test your wares, and the hungriest. It's been so long since a morsel of food has slid over my taste buds that I could eat the rattle off a snake and come back for more. Surely you must have something you want tasted by a professional taster. I'm it."

"We don't have a thing because we haven't cooked today, but I'm touched by your line of malarkey. Maybe I can find something for you. Stand by for a minute."

She returned and handed me a bag. "There's a nutritious snack for you. You can make a sandwich by putting the vegetable soup between the two slices of whole wheat bread."

"That's marvelous, miss... Now if there happens to be a little nubbin left of the loaf you cut the slices off, and you were to give it to me, I could have two sandwiches and wouldn't have to bother you again tomorrow."

She left and returned to add half a loaf of bread to my loot. "There," she said. "But with a spiel like that, how do you know we wouldn't like to have you back tomorrow?"

Hmmm, I thought, as I thanked her and walked back to the rendezvous. I wish old Jim were here. He'd know how to take advantage of a situation like this. In his absence, I ate the soft center out of the half-loaf, filled the hole thus made with condensed soup, and devoured my hearty meal as a child would gobble an ice cream cone.

I scribbled a note to Dave, informing him that Jim had gone home. I added that if I got a job and he had to wait for me, he'd find Pete's a good place to hang out, and he might mooch a meal at the Domestic Art Department of the college. Then I left for the pool hall, confident in the knowledge that, being responsible only for myself, I could cope with whatever lay before me.

113

Pete greeted me with good news. "Cy, my boy, Charlie Jackson was here a few minutes ago, looking for a stacker. I told him you'd be back and not to hire nobody till he had a chance to look you over. He's boss at the Great Dane's spread. This might mean a coupla week's work for you."

"That's good news, Pete. Do you know which way he went?"

"No, he had some errands to run. Don't get excited. He said he'd be back."

"Pete, Angus told me several things about the Sullivan farm that were handy to know when I got there. Maybe you can tell me something about the Great Dane's spread that'll get me off on the right foot?"

"Sure, there's no secret about it. John O. Pederson owns the ranch. He's a great big feller and a Dane. He worked all his life to build up the ranch but when the depression hit, it hit him hard. He took to the bottle and it got the best of him. He's an alcoholic who can't control himself. The bank, to protect its interest, convinced the Great Dane to turn the management over to his foreman. That's Charlie Jackson, a damned good man."

"Why didn't the bank foreclose on him, Pete?"

"The banks have foreclosed so many places already they've got their hands full. Besides, the bank doesn't want to be in the sheep business and they know that John O. Pederson does. They just hope he'll straighten out. They figure he's such a prince of a man it's worth a try. Here comes Angus. He knows the Great Dane and might give you some good pointers. Take him on for the house. Remember, you win two games out of three."

Angus was a storehouse of knowledge about the world in general and ranching in particular. He shared it with me as we played pool.

"Yes," he said, "I know the Great Dane's spread. It's out on the Bannack Road. Now there's a place for ya, Bannack. It's kind of a ghost town now, but it used to be the Capital of Montana Territory. It was also headquarters for the old Henry Plummer gang till the vigilantes strung 'em up. They're all

114

buried out back of Skinner's Saloon. That whole area is great sheep country."

I racked the balls. Angus caught his breath and continued. "We don't range sheep on the desert like you do down Utah-Nevada way. It's too cold here. We run 'em on the summer range, then feed 'em at the home ranch during the cold part of the winter. That means we have to put up hay and haul it to 'em. The ranches cover hundreds, maybe thousands of acres, and the prairie hay grows volunteer, We just cut and stack it, and haul it in as we need it. Takes a lot of labor when the hay is ripe and needs puttin'up. That's why we use hobo labor.

"Hire 'em when we need 'em, but we don't have no worry about their keep when we don't need 'em. Same way with horsepower. Takes a lot of horses during the busy season but not during the rest of the year. That's why we run our horses wild most of the time and re-break 'em to work during the hayin' time."

"That means the guys who do this kind of work have to know what it's all about?"

That's true about the guys handlin' half-wild horses on the mowin' machines, rakes, bull rakes, and the derrick team. On the other hand, all the stacker needs is a strong back and lots of endurance. But he gets premium pay for it, same as the foreman. And he's top dog next to the foreman."

As Angus was describing the facts of ranch life to me, two men entered the pool hall. One was John, the foreman of the Sullivan farm, and the other was a husky man of about forty. On motion from John they came to our table.

"Hello, Angus," the stranger said, before addressing me. "You must be Cy that Pete was telling me about."

"That's right, and you must be Charlie Jackson. If you need some help I'd sure like to work for you."

"Ever do any stackin?"

"I've never stacked for bull rakes, but I know the business end of a pitch fork and am plenty able."

John broke in. "Charlie, I hired him for the stack but Joe O'Toole, my regular stacker, showed up. I used him in the field a couple of days and I'd say he can hold up his end."

"That's good enough for me, John. Okay, Cy, let's shake on it."

As we shook hands casually I sensed a firmness in his grip that was more than a handshake. He was challenging me. He was showing me who was boss. As he increased the pressure, I responded. As his superior strength became evident, I countered by using technique rather than strength to cancel his advantage. I pressed my thumb firmly into the hollow between his thumb and forefinger, a trick I had learned as a boy in competition with others who were feeling their oats. This momentary exchange, this little byplay, ended in a standoff. In that brief moment we developed respect, each for the other.

En route to the Great Dane's ranch Charlie seemed preoccupied in thought. Content in my ignorance of his concerns, I thought of my own and did not probe for his. The sun set as we drove toward Bannack. The afterglow faded. and the brisk air of night descended as we drove into the yard.

Charlie roused from his reverie. "Cy, you can take the third bunkhouse from the end. But before you turn in, stick around for a bit while I check on the old man. He's so goddamn big and strong that if he's on a rampage I'll need some help."

I walked over to my assigned bunkhouse and stood at the entry while Charlie carried a box of groceries into the cookhouse. He soon came back out and gave me the high-sign to turn in. I did so with mixed emotions. Something within me, a haunting mixture of premonition and hope, wrestled for my thoughts, then foundered throughout a night of troubled sleep.

I rose early to get my bearings. The Bitterroot Mountains loomed majestically in the background. In their shadow lay the John O. Pedersen ranch, a spread of several hundred acres of volunteer hay; a cluster of barns and sheep sheds to protect sheep against the cold of winter; a homestead and, tied to it end-to-end with common walls, a large cookhouse and six small bunkhouses. Exposed in sunshine beneath a cloudless sky, the

116

landscape was graced not by tree, shrub, or flower; just prairie hay and sprawling buildings bleached by the sun, dried by the wind, and wracked by the cold of bitter winters.

Only in the quiet darkness of defeat, I thought, could men live out their lives in such desolation. I pondered further -- why am I now part of the scene? Do such forlorn surroundings lead to hopeless despair in other men? Or do they dream that some day, in some way, their time will come? Perhaps they, too, nurture their dreams on hope.

My reverie ended abruptly as Charlie came out of the homestead. "Cy, the rest of the crew'll be along pretty quick and we'll have some breakfast. We've had a crew of four men for most of a week, breakin' the range horses to work, mowin' and rakin' into windrows. Stackin's a tough job so we'll break you in easy today with just one bull rake to stack for. We'll start gradual so you can get the hang of it, and work up to two bull rakes tomorrow."

The rest of the crew joined us. We introduced ourselves all around, went into the cookhouse, and sat down at a large plank table. The cook entered. Noting a full crew, he took a sheep bell from a shelf and rang it gently a couple of times. Ceremonial ranch courtesy, I thought. The door to the homestead opened and a tremendous hulk of a man came through the opening. He manoeuvered sidewise to come through the doorway, stooped to keep from hitting his head as he came forward, and seated himself at the head of the table. Ceremonial ranch courtesy? My God, this man needs no ceremonial courtesy to command respect.

What a Great Dane he was! Massive head, prominent Roman nose, eyes a blend of cloud and fire that displayed a formidable mixture of emotion -- pride, strength, weakness, and ambition suppressed but not surrendered. He nodded recognition, "Mornin' men, heave to."

After breakfast Charlie suggested that I take it easy while he and the crew hitched up. I followed them to the barn to observe and to help if needed. The ten horses in the corral showed mounting agitation as we approached. These wiry, tough little mustangs threw their heads high and milled round and round with eyes blazing and nostrils flaring in mortal fear. Having worked with wild broncos as riding ponies on Roy Lazzenbee's ranch as a boy, I was interested in their performance under the harness. Gradually they calmed as we manoeuvered them into separate stalls in the barn.

Each man harnessed and bridled a team. The bridles were equipped with large blinders to keep the horses from spooking. Charlie helped one man hitch his team to a mowing machine, two men hitch their teams to rakes, and the fourth man his team to a bull rake. He then drove his own team, the most docile of the five, to the derrick.

For putting up hay with bull rakes, the hay is cut a few inches above ground by mowing machines, gathered into windrows by rakes, then moved to the derrick by bull rakes where it it deposited on the derrick fork. The derrick team raises the fork over the top of the derrick, and the hay drops on the other side where the stack is formed.

The function of the stacker, using a pitchfork, is to move the hay from where it dropped to form the four sides of the stack, and round off the top like a mushroom.

This is quite an operation, I thought, as we started the stack. Use of the bull rake makes unnecessary the hand labor of cocking the hay and of pitching on in the field. Just maintain a balance among the four jobs; mowing, raking, bull raking, and stacking, and this is a quick way of putting up hay. Quick did I say? Charlie said two bull rakes tomorrow. When the mowing is finished, I wonder if that means stacking for three bull rakes. When the raking is done, I wonder if that means stacking for four. Hmmm, we'll see. I'd better get toughened up for a real job of work ahead of me. Maybe that's why Charlie was so solicitous of my welfare.

My reverie was rudely interrupted. "Charlie, Charlie!" Cookee yelled, as he came running toward the stack. "Help, help, he's got the snakes."

"Goddamn it," Charlie barked, as he tied his team to the derrick. "Come on, Cy, while Cookee gathers the rest of the crew."

When the field hands saw Cookee approach, they headed for the corral to tie up their teams as though in rehearsed fire drill. They were only slightly behind Charlie and me in reaching the homestead.

"No, no, no, get outa here; out of here and leave me alone; oh, leave me alone, oooh," we heard the Great Dane coax, then moan and groan as we approached the door. He was standing on a bench, shaking violently as his trembling hands wiped beads of sweat from his forehead. On seeing us, he raved excitedly, incoherently. He waved at the far corner of the room, jumped to the floor, and ran wildly through the door.

Powerful beast of a man though he was, he was unable to escape the six of us. We subdued him physically and, although unable to allay his mental anguish, we part carried, part dragged him into the "snake house."

The snake house was the first bunkhouse in the line adjoining the cookhouse. Charlie had reinforced it to withstand the violence of a bull and had padded it all around to protect the Great Dane when suffering delirium tremens. The poor man was now in that state. In his irrational thought and confused speech, he alternately beseeched the snakes to go away and cajoled Charlie to let him out.

Charlie responded, "Sorry, boss, sorry. We can't let you out till suppertime. You'll be all right by them. Okay, boss? Cookee, is dinner ready? It's about that time. We'll have a bite to eat, then get back on the job."

Work progressed smoothly that afternoon. I figured out a couple of things about stacking for bull rakes that were good to know as the job progressed. First, if I allowed the hay to build up a bit and overflow the place where it landed, I wouldn't have such a chore in moving it to the sides of the stack. Second, if I didn't make such a large stack, I wouldn't have to carry the hay so far. And, besides, I'd have more rest breaks because we'd have to move the derrick more often.

I topped out the stack late in the afternoon and we moved the derrick to a new site. On this stack I allowed the hay to build up where it had fallen, then framed it into considerably smaller stacks. As we quit for the day, Charlie moved alongside me and said with a grin, "Cy, you learn quick, don't you? I think you'll get along. Wash up with the crew at the watering trough and I'll see if the old man is fit to leave the snake house."

Apparently Charlie found the Great Dane fit. He was seated at the table when we entered the cookhouse at the sound of the dinner bell. His utter dejection bade us be quiet as he hesitated before signalling us to pass the food, family style, and begin the meal.

His brooding eyes showed desire for understanding. Not for lack of sympathy but for lack of words were we unable to break the spell of gloom. In silent contemplation, we ate dinner and retired to our separate bunks.

Next morning at breakfast the Great Dane showed no ill effect from his drunken orgy. Later, as we were harnessing the teams, I commented to Charlie that the old man had made a marvelous recovery from his bout with the bottle. He thought for a moment, then leveled with me. "It's not a recovery, Cy; it's just a lull in the storm. I keep hoping he'll get so goddamn sick he'll quit, but he doesn't. He fights a battle every day and I'm sorry to say he loses every round. Some days he lasts till noon. Some days he doesn't. But every day, sooner or later, we'll have to lock him up in the snake house. That's the way it is."

I was thankful that Charlie had broken me in gradually by stacking for just one bull rake, as muscles not normally used were brought into play. My legs were particularly lame because in carrying forkloads to the fringes of the stack, at each step I sank deep into the loosely packed hay. Every morning I felt as weary and stiff as after the first football scrimmage of the season. But as the work progressed and the days passed, a combination of increased skill and tougher body brought new delight. I was sorry to see the job coming to an end.

On the last day, all the hay was cut and raked. Charlie assigned Spike, one of the field hands, to work with me on the stack and the other three to drive bull rakes. About mid morning, our routine was broken by Charlie's frantic shout, "Help! Cy, Spike, Help!"

As I slid off the stack, Charlie was trying to control his derrick team with one hand and motion me to help Red with the other. Red's horses, for some reason, had been sparked. Red, striving to control them, had fallen, helplessly entangled between his team and the bull rake. If either team had lurched, Red could have lost a leg.

I grabbed the bridle of one of Red's horses. Spike, having slid off the far side of the stack, grabbed the other. By that time the other two field hands had arrived. One of them controlled both teams and the other unhitched Red's team from the bull rake. Red, visibly shaken, extricated himself. We all heaved a sigh of relief.

Dinner that night was more jovial than usual, perhaps from a common sense of satisfaction for a job well done. More likely, it was from a sense of comradeship that showed only when one of us was rescued by concerted action of the others.

Charlie paid us off and offered to take us to town, either that night or after breakfast the next morning, whichever we wanted. I agreed with the others that we should start out in the morning on a full stomach.

When paying us off, Charlie offered me a full time job helping him with the sheep. I said I'd think on it over night and let him know. My earlier experience working with sheep hadn't been all bad. However, it had convinced me that there must be a better life than that of a sheepherder. The Great Dane tried to find a better life through recourse to the bottle. He created not a better life, but need for a greater search, a search for sanity.

The more I thought about Charlie's offer, the more I realized how confused and uncertain I was. Had I not left home in search of work, work of any kind? Or was my journey a quest for work that offered hope for a better life? Should I grasp this opportunity to work when it is offered? Or should I continue my quest for something better? Does this opportunity to work lead to a better life? No. Does it offer hope? No. Hope has carried me this far. I'll not abandon it.

In the morning I said, "Charlie, thanks for the job offer but I think I'll move along. I'll see you next year if I'm still riding the rattlers."

# Chapter 11

# Hello Butte. Good-bye Boodle Town

When Charlie dropped me off in Dillon, I went directly to our boxcar rendezvous. I was pleased to find Dave there, and was suddenly overcome with emotion. Temporary friendships struck with fellow workers were hollow substitutes for my deep and abiding affection for my brother. We had shared hardship and elation all our lives. There could be no greater bond between us. We eagerly recounted our adventures.

"My job in the pea harvest was for only a few days," Dave said. "I stretched it into a couple of weeks by making myself useful. In addition to a five-acre pea patch, that farmer had a big garden to take care of his family needs.

"When I saw the eight children, each needing a haircut the worst way, I remembered how pleased Mrs. Jensen was when I cut her boys' hair back in Blackfoot. When I started cutting these kids' hair, I stopped to cogitate. If I clip just one each day, that'll give me eight day's work. I had it figured right. By the time I finished shearing 'em all, the old feller was mighty pleased. I'd done a good job weeding his garden and sprucing up his yard so he kept me on for a few extra days. How about you?"

I told him of our brief stint at the Sullivan farm, of Jim's leaving, my experiences at the Great Dane's ranch, and my turning down Charlie's offer of a steady job. He agreed that no matter how tempting dead-end work might be, we should accept it for the present only.

"While waiting for you," Dave said, "I absorbed a bit of hobo lore from an old timer who shared the boxcar with me one night. Next morning that fellow heated some water, lathered his face with laundry soap, broke a quart Mason jar against a rock, and shaved with a fragment that had broken to his liking. He then rinsed his face, squeezed a ribbon of shaving cream from a tube, and applied it as lotion.

"When I questioned this strange procedure he said, 'I've shaved this way for years and never cut myself yet. Shavin' cream's a no-good shavin' soap, but it's a damn good lotion. Try it some time.'

"The fruit harvest in Washington isn't ripe for picking," Dave continued. "Although some work is available at the orchards in the Yakima Valley, we'll have a better chance on the wheat harvest in the Dakotas. If we go east out of Butte, we'd better take the Milwaukee Road. That's short for the Chicago, Milwaukee, St. Paul, & Pacific. The other eastbound line, the Great Northern, has been cracking down on transients. They've always had yard bulls and now they have riding bulls on every freight. A few vandals take advantage of a free ride. They break the seals on boxcars, steal like pack rats, and raise hell in general. You can't blame the railroads for getting tough, but it sure hurts the rest of us."

We decided to try our luck in Butte and take it from there. "Let's figure out our schedule," Dave said. "I've found a good place to eat. It's called the Cabbage Patch Cafe. It's part of an old barn in the middle of an abandoned cabbage patch. It's a family venture. Mama's the cook, papa's the clean-up man, and their daughter's the waitress.

"This family was driving through town with all their belongings in a beat-up truck when they saw this deserted plot. They leased it and planted a few vegetables to have something to eat. When they realized that farming is just a slow way of starving, they fixed up one part of the barn as a cafe. Now they've got cows for milk and meat, chickens for eggs, and a garden for vegetables – all for use in their cafe.

"They charge fifteen cents for all you can eat. That's typically a hamburger steak, boiled potatoes and gravy, bread and butter, and whatever vegetable might be in season. The all-you-can-eat feature is the potatoes and gravy part. While waiting for you, I've survived nicely on one meal a day. I wait till I'm mighty hungry, about two o'clock. Then for fifteen cents, I really fill up. That lasts me till the next day. Let's do our errands, have a good feed this afternoon at the Cabbage Patch Cafe, then take the afternoon freight north."

Dave had explored Dillon so he knew where to find bargains. We purchased a change of clothes, a toothbrush and a spoon for each of us, a pocket knife for me, a set of barber tools for Dave, a pound of coffee, a bar of laundry soap, and a pair of buckskin shoe laces to tie up our bundles. Where we had knives and spoons, we reasoned, we didn't need forks; and the smaller our bundles, the better. Instead of carrying tooth powder to clean our teeth, we'd use salt, soap, or powdered charcoal from the ashes of a fire.

"We shouldn't look too prosperous or we'll get rolled," Dave said, "so we'd better boil our new clothes. While we're at it, we might as well boil 'em all, take a bath, and start out fresh."

After our cleanup campaign we cut the stitching at the waist band of our Levis. Each of us tucked in two one-dollar bills, so if we got rolled we wouldn't lose our bankroll. We retained some pocket change, sent the balance of our earnings to our mother in a postal money order, and drifted over to the cafe.

The Cabbage Patch Cafe was functional and clean. Mama the cook, in gingham dress with matching apron, was at the stove and counter at one end of the room. Papa the cleanup man, in well washed butcher's garb, was at one of the tables scrubbing imaginary soil from its stark surface. Daughter the waitress, in white blouse and checkered red and white skirt, was in the background, quietly serving four men at one of the six tables in the dining area. We approached another customer who was sitting alone at another table.

"Mind if we join you?" we greeted him.

"Don't mind if ya do," he answered. "Sometimes I like company. You ever been here before? It's a good place, but they always serve more than a man can eat. I hate to see it wasted nowadays."

There was only one item on the menu so the waitress didn't wait for our order. She served us hamburger steak with the fixings. Our companion surveyed his meal, cut his steak down

125

the middle, pushed half of it to the edge of his plate, and started to eat. As we neared the end of the meal Dave eyed that piece of steak and asked, "What are you going to do with that left-over steak?"

"Nothing. Do you want it?"

"I sure enough do," Dave said, and thanked the man as he slid half his hamburger steak onto Dave's plate. Dave shared his bounty with me. After second helpings we felt fortified for the day. As we were leaving the cafe Dave asked the cook if she could spare a little pepper mixed with some salt. She obliged by filling a Bull Durham bag that Dave provided. We paid our bill, left a ten cent tip, and left for Butte, Montana.

Having been reared in a mining camp, Dave and I were well versed in the lore of the mining industry. We were familiar with, and practitioners of, the jargon of the mining fraternity. Within that fraternity the vocabulary is specific and the breach of it a sure sign of a newcomer to the trade. Although young in years, we were old-timers in use of the language. That familiarity enabled us to establish easy comradeship with a boomer who boarded our boxcar in Melrose soon after our train left Dillon.

A boomer miner is one with itchy feet. He plies his trade in one mining district until he gets bored, or goes on a binge and blows his bankroll. He takes to the rails for another camp and there repeats the process. Over time he works in many of the major mining camps of the West. His experience in a variety of mining methods gains him a job wherever he applies. He holds a job for as long as he can control his thirst and wanderlust.

Our boomer friend assumed we were of his tradition and soon opened up. "I've been workin' open-pit down in Ruth, Nevada, but I don't like that kind of work. If a man's got miner's blood in his veins he can't make it on top of the ground. He's like a mole. He can find his way around by the kind of rock he's in, but that damned wind and sunshine don't make no sense.

"I've worked Butte before, but I'm going back till winter sets in. Then I'll head for Arizona and try the Magma mine. They tell me it's hotter'n hell in the Magma mine, but I want to see for myself.

126

"Now Butte, she's a great town," our comrade continued. "She's wide open and they pay good wages. I guess they pay good 'cause the union's gettin' strong. It's gotta be strong or the company would ride all over 'em. The Anaconda Company's got a good thing. Butte's the richest hill on earth, and the company milks it like a cow. Right now the price of copper's way down and lots of miners are out of work. The company don't give a damn about miners; they just mine enough high-grade to pay salaries of the high-muckie-mucks. It's a shame they can't fall back on somethin' besides copper.

"Butte was first a gold mining camp, and a rich one. When the old-timers dug below the enriched gold zone they encountered silver, and Butte became a rich silver camp. When they mined below the oxidized zone the silver petered out and they hit good copper ore. Now it's a great copper camp. It's a shame they have to depend on copper during this depression."

"On another subject," I asked, "is Butte as tough a boodle town as it's cracked up to be? Should we be concerned?"

"I'm not concerned about it," he said, "but I'm not concerned about anything. If you're worried and like your freedom, you better hop off at Silver Bow and hike the road into Butte."

We hiked the highway. The scene, as we approached the city, was dominated by headframes surrounded by waste dumps. Abandoned workings, scattered like gopher holes, were evidence of early day failures. Huge glory holes were evidence of latter day success. These scars of surface subsidence were evidence of the magnitude of underground mining. The scope of this man-made empire, set in the midst of nature's mountain ranges, was overwhelming.

The plight of the city itself was in sad contrast to the glory days of the past, a reflection of the depth to which the depression had degraded life. Men jostled in a queue snaking around the block, checking a rumor that one of the mines was hiring. Gambling casinos with loaded dice catered to a few sharks and many suckers trying in quiet desperation to beat the game.

127

Although our efforts to remain inconspicuous had been well planned, we soon found ourselves objects of the sheriff's interest. Apparently our bundles first attracted his attention. Stopping his patrol car to question us, he saw from our sunburned faces that we were strangers to his domain, and probably transients subject to his authority.

"What are you boys doing here?"

"Just passing through."

"You got any money or visible means of support?"

"We don't have folding money, but we're able." We showed him our calloused hands.

"If you don't have five dollars apiece, you're subject to our vagrancy laws. Come with me and we'll see the judge."

The judge was as perfunctory as the sheriff had been, and more businesslike. He shuffled some papers, examined his register, and mused half aloud. "Hmmm. Guess we've got room for two more. Men, if you haven't got five dollars apiece you're vagrants as charged. Do you plead guilty or not guilty?"

We pled guilty. The judge sentenced us to five days in the county jail. We signed some papers he passed to us. The sheriff drove us to the county jail, stored our bundles, and locked us up.

There were about thirty cells in the jail but only eight inmates. With the jail so sparsely filled, we pondered the judge's comment, "Guess we've got room for two more." We learned the reason at supper time when the Kangaroo Court was convened. A Kangaroo Court is a mock tribunal devised by prisoners to maintain order among themselves, to establish seniority, and to force deference by recent inmates to their seniors. The judge of the court is by custom the one who has served longest in the jail.

After extracting two-bits each from Dave and me, as entrance fee into the club, the judge explained the facts of life. "Me and four other guys are being held for hearings, so they've got to hold us. You and three other guys on vagrancy charges will have a fancy supper of beans, a bunk in a cell, and a breakfast of gruel. Then the sheriff will come to you, real friendly like, and offer to take you to the edge of town if you want to vamoose. Of course you want to get out of this goddamn boodle town pronto. So you vamoose, and nobody's around to question the nice little racket the sheriff and the judge have got going for them.

"It's really a smooth racket," the judge of the Kangaroo Court continued. "The sheriff has the feeding concession. He gets paid a buck a day for every prisoner of record. It costs maybe two-bits for the grub so he makes six-bits a head on us steady customers.

"The big deal is where they round up you guys as vagrants and give you five days in the clink. You're on the record for five days so the sheriff gets five bucks and you're here only one night. He and the judge are in cahoots, so they split the proceeds of the feeding concession and work things out to keep the jailhouse full according to the record. The judge certifies the record and makes you sign it when you're sentenced. Isn't that a sweet racket? I think when I get out of here I'll run for sheriff, where I know all about the office."

We ate our supper of bread, beans, and tepid coffee, and slept fitfully on iron cots fastened to the floor. After breakfast of oatmeal mush and coffee, the sheriff made his rounds. "If you boys have learned your lesson and want to get out of town I'll give you a break. I'll take you to the outskirts of town if you'll keep right on going."

The sheriff was considerate enough to release us near the yards of the Milwaukee Road, and to provide some useful advice. "You'll go through several tunnels crossing the divide. It's a steep grade and they use three or four locomotives on these long freights. Get up front, right back of the lead engines, or the smoke and soot in those tunnels will make you wish you was back in jail."

We looked for an empty boxcar but found none. Several hoboes were primed to board some flatcars loaded with redwood logs. We judged that they, too, had found no empties so further search would be fruitless. As the train highballed out of the yard we climbed the grab irons and manoeuvered to the deck of one of the boxcars near the lead locomotive. From this perch we watched as Butte faded into the background.

As we climbed upward toward the Continental Divide, the seemingly endless train slowly rounded hairpin curves. In the distance far below it appeared as a sinuous snake. In the foreground it seemed an articulated caterpillar. Ahead lay the tunnels about which the sheriff had warned us. In passing through them we got dirty with smoke, but not nearly so grimy as we would have been if riding far back on the train. We felt fortunate to have had the advice of the sheriff. He had been a scalawag who looked after his own interest at the expense of ours, but he had been considerate, too, and we were thankful for that.

The train lumbered over the Continental Divide and gained speed as it moved eastward on the gentler side of the Rocky Mountains. Three Forks was a major junction, so we left the train while cars were shifted about. A friendly switchman told us, "This train will leave in an hour or so on the southern route through Bozeman and Billings. A later train will follow the northern route through Harlowton. The two lines meet at Miles City."

We bought a can of soup and a loaf of bread at a neighborhood store, devoured them, and headed for Billings. Being unable to find an empty boxcar, we resumed our perch on the deck of what was now "our" boxcar.

The top of a boxcar is slightly convex to facilitate runoff of rain water. The deck is a platform made of hardwood planks. It is about two feet wide and extends the length of the boxcar. Our perch was relatively clean because we had been lying on it all the way from Butte. We felt a proprietary interest in this car. Further, it was a heavily loaded boxcar which rolled smoothly over the rails rather than bumpity-bump as do empties. We felt an attachment for this old friend.

Riding the top of a boxcar clipping along at fifty or sixty miles an hour is frightening. The deck provides the only support. One must stay awake and maintain firm grasp of it. To stay awake hour after hour, mile after mile, without succumbing to the hypnotic influence of the swaying, undulating boxcar presents a continuing problem. Dave and I lay prone, side by side, head to the wind, each with one arm around the other and a firm grip on the edge of the outside planks with the other arm. In this position either of us could doze, but unusual movement of one would alert the other.

**Two hobos riding the deck of a boxcar, feeling as insignificant back of the locomotive as they appear in the drawing**

Lying in one position for a long time is frustrating. Occasional shifting about is necessary. There is relief in change, even though it be from bad to worse, and it is comforting to shift one's position and be bruised in a different place. We manoeuvered to exchange positions from time to time, and in consequence developed roughly an equivalence of bruises.

As the train approached the Bozeman yards we saw several hoboes in a makeshift jungle. We decided to find a place where we could stretch out in comfort for the night. Available in the jungle were wood, water, and an assortment of pans. We heated some water in a large container, took baths, dressed in our clean change of clothes, and placed our dirty ones in the container to boil up while we studied the situation.

We had half a loaf of bread saved from lunch, but we needed something substantial. Ideally we should provide some leftovers for the next day. We had resolved to spend no more than twenty cents a day on food. Why not a Mulligan stew with baked potatoes on the side? For our stew we needed meat and vegetables. I set out for town to buy some stewing meat. Dave left for the nearest farmhouse to cut some hair in trade for vegetables. When we returned to the campfire I had a doggy bone and two-bits worth of meat, for which I had spent a dime. Dave had carrots, onions, and potatoes, for which he had cut two heads of hair.

While the marrow was cooking out of the bone we diced and added the stew meat and vegetables, made a pot of coffee, rinsed, wrung, and hung out our boiled clothes to dry, and settled in for a hearty meal. Dave had brought extra potatoes. We jacketed four of them in mud packs and covered them with hot ashes to bake overnight for survival fare the next day. We had a good meal, a sound sleep near the campfire, and a breakfast of leftover Mulligan stew. That was an excellent start for our next lap to Billings.

As we examined the outbound freight to find a good place to ride, Dave's attention riveted on a refrigerated boxcar. "Look at that reefer, Cy. The hatch isn't closed. Maybe she's not hauling perishables. If not, there's no ice in the compartment and we can ride in there instead of on the deck."

Sure enough, there was no ice in the compartment. We inched down into it, and made sure the hatch didn't close behind us. Hoboes in the jungle had told of being locked for days in the ice compartment of reefers. We wanted no part of that. Although the grating on which we snuggled was rougher than the deck, it was tolerable, and we enjoyed protection from the elements. An amiable north wind on the ground loses its amiability to someone riding the top of a boxcar. We had had enough for the present of amiable north winds.

As we settled into the ice compartment, the space available seemed ample for comfort. We were happy to be protected from the elements and content not to stand or move about freely. Comfort is a relative term, however, and with the passage of time we felt increasingly confined in our huddled positions. Loss in freedom of movement bred fear and anxiety. "What if" imaginings spawned panic. At the first stop we flung open the hatch, made a hasty exit from that devilish confinement, and left the train. We wanted our feet on the ground, no matter where that ground might be.

# Chapter 12

## Any Kind of Work

*Oh, why don't you work*
*Like other men do?*
  *How the hell can I work*
*When there's no work to do?*
  *Hallelujah, I'm a bum;*
*Hallelujah, bum again.*

As Dave rendered that plaintive refrain of the hobo, I thought about our own plight. We are not so different. Other men don't find work either. We've seen them on street corners and skid row, in hobo jungles and soup kitchens. We've joined them riding the rails aimlessly from place to place, seeking not the treasure at the end of a rainbow, but the means of survival. How the hell can I work when there's no work to do? Hallelujah, I'm a bum; Hallelujah, bum again. Damn it.

We rode the reefer from Bozeman to Columbus, Montana, a railroad town. A shopping center for the surrounding villages and ranches, it was as good a place as any to look for work. Fortified with a lunch of baked potatoes, we explored the town. One store displayed glue-on rubber soles at fifteen cents a pair. Our shoes had worn thin so we bought some soles and glued them on. We learned at the store that work might be found at one of the ranches in Absorakee, a town some distance to the south. We struck out on the highway and soon picked up a ride.

Albert, the farmer who stopped for us, apparently did so at the urging of his wife. "Climb in the back seat," he growled. His old Chalmers was more or less the worse for wear, but it had been a fine car in its day and we climbed in. His wife Martha, sitting next to him, was outgoing and eager for an audience. Before long we knew their history and their problems.

135

Martha was tall, lean, and rangy. Her wide mouth, set in a bony face, housed a tongue that chattered incessantly. As she vented her pentup wisdom to a fresh audience, her husband didn't listen; he knew what she was saying. Albert, evidently accustomed to playing second fiddle to his formidable wife, nodded agreement from time to time, then withdrew into a somber shell.

"Albert and I can make do," she said. "We never knew real prosperity. We just tightened our belts when things got tougher. All we've got is a survival farm. That's a relative word. Our kind of survival wasn't good enough for our two boys when they grew up, so they joined the CCC's. That's the Civilian Conservation Corps, you know. They get their food and clothes, and make thirty dollars a month. Can't say that I blame them for leaving. We couldn't pay wages like that. We did well to keep them in meat and potatoes. So here we are. Albert needs help, and we can't afford to hire any. Things just go down hill."

"Maybe we could help you out for a few days," Dave suggested. "We wouldn't need any pay, just our food. That way you could have help when you need it most, and we could look around for a paying job in our spare time, if we have any."

Albert came out of his shell. "Martha, can you feed 'em for a few days? With some help I can pour a concrete footing under the corner of the barn that's slumping so bad."

"I guess we can find something to eat," she said, "and they can sleep in the boys' room."

After several days respite from hard labor, Dave and I were eager to get to work. Albert had all the paraphernalia usually found on isolated farmsteads, including the tools necessary for the job at hand. We jacked up the corner of the barn, removed the original rock support, and dug down to a solid base to support a concrete footing. By the end of the day we were hungry and weary. After taking a splashing good bath in the watering trough we donned our clean clothes in anticipation of meat and potatoes for supper.

Martha served meat and potatoes embellished with many of the delicacies normally reserved for Thanksgiving dinner. Dave and I showed our appreciation by eating prodigiously. Albert showed concern at the disappearance in one meal of goodies that would normally be shared by him and Martha over a period of weeks. His increasing testiness cast a cloud over our spirits. After helping Martha with the dishes we retired.

As we were coming down the stairway next morning we hesitated because of an argument in the kitchen. "No, Martha, we'll finish the barn today, give 'em breakfast tomorrow, then turn 'em loose."

"But, Albert, you've got a lot of work that needs doing. They don't expect pay for their work, just their meals."

"I know that, but we just can't afford it."

Dave and I made some scuffling noises before entering the kitchen. The argument ceased, but during breakfast the sense of unresolved antagonism remained. We managed to clear the atmosphere by announcing that if we finished work on the barn we would leave next morning and look for a paying job. Our hosts were relieved to have their differences settled amicably.

The conversation we had heard, however, raised questions. "My God, Dave, is our labor not worth the grub we eat? Are times so tough and food so scarce we're not worth our keep? If that's the case this country needs a big dose of caster oil."

"It needs more than that, Cy. What keeps us going is hope. There's nothing wrong with these old people. They're proud, but they've just given up hope. They've had a rough life and I can't blame them. But goddamn it, we can't give up hope. That's all we've got. Let's go to work."

We jacked up the corner of the barn and framed in a retaining form. We mixed cement with sand and gravel, then water. With the wet concrete thus mixed, we filled the form full to the sills of the faulty section of the barn. To finish the job, Albert had only to remove the jacks after the concrete had set.

The day was young, so we helped on chores that Albert would have difficulty performing alone. After a substantial breakfast the next morning, we left for the Anderson ranch a few miles farther south. Martha had told us the life history of Matt Anderson, so we knew what to expect. We left Albert and

Martha knowing that sometimes, when the going gets rough, women are stronger than men.

\* \* \* \*

Matt Anderson was an enterprising farmer. His large yard was neatly arranged with a chicken coop and stables at the rear, granaries on one side, and farm implements on the other. Our attention focused first on a huge steam engine tractor, then on a threshing machine. Aha, threshing requires manpower. Maybe we're in luck.

**A steam engine means work is in the offing**

Behind the house was a large shed. Flashes from a welding torch indicated activity, so we approached the two men inside and introduced ourselves. Matt Anderson said, "I'll finish patching up this binder, then we'll talk."

Judging from the appearance of Matt's shop and farmstead, he was a competent and versatile man. We found, in working for him, that his relative prosperity was due to a combination of common sense and high aspiration. Having no children, he devoted himself to his wife, his house, and his farm. With slight formal education, he developed his talents through study of bulletins and discussions with the County Agricultural Agent.

Matt was a man worth knowing. From machining to blacksmithing and welding, from carpentry to electrical and plumbing repair, he was able within his own shop to keep his

138

house and equipment in top condition. As we were sizing up his shop he was looking us over. Upon finishing his job he turned to us.

"The busy season is coming up, so I'll need some help. Did you ever run binders?"

"No, but you show us once and we can run 'em. Hitch 'em to tractors or horses. Doesn't matter. And we know which is the business end of a pitchfork."

"That's good. I pay six-bits a day and found. My wife is a good cook, so the found is worth more than the pay. Take it easy today and explore around the farm and ask questions. The more you know the more help you'll be. Besides, you might have an idea or two that I can use. If you do, speak up. Now let's go over to the house and meet Ma. Everybody calls her Ma, she's so motherly."

Ma's cordiality showed in every line and laugh wrinkle in her chubby face. Her dapple gray hair was fine in texture and prematurely sparse. She wore it nestled in a bun. Her eyes seemed inquisitive at first, then soft and knowing. She wiped her hands on an apron tied round her ample girth. "First I'll show you the bunks and where the washroom is. After you freshen up, come back and we'll have a cup of coffee and something more if you're hungry."

We declined the "something more" and hesitated to attack her homemade raised doughnuts. She insisted, "Come on now, nobody ever got fat eating just one doughnut. Ha." So we each had a delicious doughnut with our coffee. Dave was eager to examine the farm implements we would be using, so he left. I was fascinated by Ma's kitchen activities, so I tarried.

"Deer have been raising the devil with apple orchards around here lately," Ma said. "One of the neighbors knocked one over yesterday and shared it with us. I'm making mincemeat out of the head and neck. There's nothing like venison to make good mincemeat."

"I see you have a Universal food chopper mounted on the counter. I used to twist the crank of one just like it for my mother. Can I give you a hand?"

She cut and pulled the meat off the bones, and fed it into the food chopper as I turned the crank. "Hmmm," she said, "about four quarts. That's pretty good."

She transferred the chopped meat to a large canner and added the cider in which she had cooked it. As I cranked the chopper she added eight apples, about a quart of suet, three boxes of raisins, three oranges, and three lemons, skins and all. She stirred that mixture, then added a quart each of molasses, vinegar, and grape juice; two tablespoons each of cinnamon, cloves, nutmeg, and salt; and a bit of pepper. "Now," she said, "comes the tasting part. As it simmers I'll add whatever jams and jellies I can spare. If it still needs sweetening I'll add some sugar. Come back in about three hours and help me sample it."

I helped clean up the kitchen and joined Dave in the yard. "Come take a look at these binders," he said. "The idea is, they cut the wheat close to the ground and tie it into bundles a foot or so in diameter. We'll run the binders a few days then come back and stand the bundles upright, ten bundles to a shock. We want to position the shocks handy to pitch onto both sides of the wagon. As long as the grain is in shocks the rain will drain off. It can sit there for weeks without spoiling. When it's convenient they can thresh it out. Let's walk over to the pasture."

There we saw six horses and a couple of colts, which prompted my question, "Why does he keep horses?"

"I wondered too. Matt told me that since he had to have riding horses to get around a spread-out farm, he might as well have a breed that could work too. Since he has horses that can work, he has to figure whether it's cheaper to use 'em on certain jobs or pay for gasoline to run his tractors. 'In this case,' he told me, 'we'll hitch horses to the binders.' It makes sense. By the way, Matt doesn't like to be called Mister Anderson, he's just plain Matt."

We moseyed along to the kitchen. "About time," Ma said. "I made some popover cookies with mincemeat filling and they're about ready. If you want to help, just feed the mincemeat to these jars." The quart Mason jars were upside-down on shallow pans of boiling water. As she righted them we filled them, screwed on caps, and placed them in a pressure cooker for twenty minutes of steaming. Then on to mincemeat-filled cookies. Ummm, good. We wrote a letter to mother, boiled up our clothes, and were ready for work the next day.

At breakfast Matt explained that threshing was a community affair. Each farmer helped the others and made his equipment and manpower available for the common good. Weather was the important thing, but as long as grain was in the shock there was no need for worry; it would be taken care of before snowfall.

Dave had familiarized himself with the operation of binders. Matt helped us harness the teams. Soon we were old hands at the job. As the afternoon wore on, Matt motioned for us to come on in. "I'm not worried about you fellows working yourselves to death. You'll have plenty of chance to do that when we start threshing. I'm thinking about my horses. Let's not overdo it."

After three days working binders and three days pitching bundles into shocks, we wondered what would come next. Matt announced that we would move the thresher to a neighbor's spread. With the steam engine as a tractor, Matt and Joe, his regular helper, positioned the threshing machine so the straw would be blown directly into the barn. With small farm tractors Dave and I followed, pulling wagons that resembled hay racks.

"Zack," Matt said to his neighbor, "we're ready to go. Joe and I will take care of the steam engine and the thresher. When the barn is full we'll move to wherever you want the straw stacks. You handle the crew."

"All right," Zack said to his friends and neighbors and their several children, "we'll start out one way and then shift around from time to time so nobody gets the dirty end of the stick. You six fellows start with the rack-wagons. You four spike pitch in the field. You two help pitch to the thresher. You two haul the grain away. You two help them unload at the granary. Little Zack, you keep everybody supplied with lemonade and fruit juice. I'll be the boss."

Everybody knew what to do. We all labored together with determination and energy. To work and strain and sweat, to drive muscles to the limit of endurance, then to relax while

141

waiting for the next stint of work -- this was glorious. To know that others, too, felt exultation in accomplishment -- this was pure delight. Delightful, too, was our noonday meal.

Not less hectic than our labors at the thresher, but more festive, were the kitchen activities of the women from the neighborhood. Throughout the morning they had arrived, each bringing her own specialty food in great amount. They knew from experience, as Dave and I were soon to learn, that the true meaning of thresher's appetite was insatiable appetite. The capacity of these men for food, born through the expenditure of prodigious energy, enhanced by the sun and open air, seemed limitless.

That noonday meal, called dinner, and the evening meal, called supper, were typical of all those served, whichever farm the threshing crew visited. Typical except that each farm wife tried to outdo those who had served as hostess before. "If Molly served two kinds of pie, I'll serve three" -- that sort of thing. All members of the threshing crew were happy beneficiaries of this friendly neighborhood competition.

After a couple of weeks Dave and I asked Matt if we could draw twenty dollars in a check made out to our mother. "Hmmm, that figures," he said, and he handed us the check. We enclosed it with long letters explaining our happy situation. Unknown to us, Ma Anderson had noted our mother's address and had written a letter to her, extolling the virtues of her sons. We learned later of the pleasure this thoughtful gesture by one motherly soul had brought to another.

After three more weeks of strenuous labor, we were sad to see that all the grain in the neighborhood was threshed and we were no longer needed. We had grown fond of Matt and Ma. They had treated us like sons and we felt like sons. Ma gave us a sack of sandwiches, fruit, and popover mincemeat cookies that would sustain us for a few days. We were leaving not as cast-offs, but as valued friends. Matt stood awkwardly with hands in back pockets and a straw toothpick in his mouth. "So long, boys. Come back next year." Dave and I said good-bye, and headed for

142

Minneapolis by way of Columbus and Miles City, Montana. We were on our way.

*   *   *   *

As Dave and I were prowling the fringe of the railroad yard at Columbus, studying the train activity, a fellow in his mid-thirties approached us. "If you guys are going east you might as well relax for a coupla hours. This train's got a defective car, what we call a badorder, that has to be fixed. The crew decided it couldn't wait till they hit Laurel, so they're gonna fix it here. My name's MacPherson."

"Thanks, Mac. If we can find a can maybe we'll have time for a cup of coffee." We took an immediate shine to this fellow. Judging from his remark and the long billed cap and striped shirt he was wearing, he was a railroader. We had found railroaders to be a pretty good lot.

"Come right this way," he said, and led us to a small jungle. "I don't have coffee, but I've got a pot. I always carry a coffee pot and plenty of sugar." We boiled a pot of coffee and sat down for a chat.

He was friendly in a reserved way and remarkedly clean for a man who had been riding a freight train for hours. We shared with him some of Ma Anderson's goodies.

"I was a switchman on the Milwaukee Road till I got bumped," he said. "I'm going back to Minneapolis. I know the ropes on this line. Maybe I can help you along the way."

Mac took a sack of sugar from his bindle, added four spoonfuls to his coffee and handed the bag to us. Second time around on the coffee he added four spoonfuls again. Dave was curious: "Why don't you stir your coffee?"

"I don't like it too sweet."

"Oh."

Oh, well, it was his sugar.

The goodies and coffee with sugar seemed to lubricate Mac's vocal chords, as did his recognition of a responsive audience. "There's no sense looking for an empty boxcar on this train," he said. "I've looked her over and the best chance we've

143

got is on flatcars loaded with Douglas Fir logs. Laurel and Billings are both major junctions so we'll have layovers there. It's a long haul but we oughta make Miles City today, Aberdeen tomorrow, and Minneapolis the next day. These towns all have good jungles."

"That sounds good to me," Dave said. "What's the chance to pick up a little work along the way? We hear the Dakotas are great wheat country. How about Aberdeen?"

"I was raised a little west of Aberdeen, and I'd say the chances are pretty slim. Down in Kansas, and especially in Iowa, they get thirty or more bushels to the acre. In South Dakota they might get eight or ten if the rains come right. All they've got is lots of flat land, so to increase their yield they keep plowing more and more of it up. The hell of it is, when they plow up the grass land, the wind blows away the topsoil. More and more you see dust storms raising hell with the land.

"Another big problem," Mac continued, "is the damned prairie dogs. If a rancher leaves his acreage in grass, the prairie dogs eat the grass and there's not much left for livestock. These damned rodents are prolific breeders. The only way to keep them under control is poison. But the poison also kills the ferrets, and the ferret is the only predator that keeps the prairie dog population under control. So I think the combination of dust storms and prairie dogs makes South Dakota an unlikely place to find work."

In our developing respect for Mac's judgment, we followed his lead and spent one night with him at each of the jungles in Miles City, Aberdeen, and Minneapolis. En route we supplemented Ma Anderson's "lunch" with purchases of bread, liverwort, and cheese; then some prunes to counteract the cheese.

Although we were flush with pay from our threshing labors, we nevertheless stretched our nickels. Instead of buying bread at grocery stores, we bought day-old punk at bakeries and usually managed to get a twenty-ounce loaf for four cents. When I looked longingly at the groceries back of a counter, and zeroed in on the most likely bargain, I was seldom disappointed in

144

making a penny-saving purchase. If there were a dime's worth of liverwort on the end of a ring and I asked for a nickel's worth, what merchant could look at my yearning expression and resist giving me the whole piece? None. And my pride was intact.

As the train slowed upon approaching the Minneapolis yards, Mac motioned for us to pile off and led us to what he called The Minnie Jungle. This was known as the finest jungle in the West, and judging from its appearance it deserved that distinction. It had all the amenities a hobo could ask for: running water, campfire sites, a few trees, a bit of grass, firewood, and space for relative privacy.

As a former worker in Minneapolis, Mac expressed hometown pride in these facilities. "Hoboes used to prowl all over town till the locals realized it would be better to provide a place for them," he said. "The jungle now keeps them out of town and gives 'em a chance to clean up without worrying about the law. Hoboes appreciate it. They keep it clean and the Sanitation Department helps out where necessary. Let's clean ourselves up."

We took possession of a campsite on the fringe of the jungle, heated water in an old double boiler, bathed, shaved, boiled our dirty clothes, and contemplated our supper.

"Let's have a real feed," I said, as I struck out for the nearest market. I returned with a dozen eggs for a dime, a loaf of bread and a chunk of salt pork for a nickel each, and three potatoes for nothing. Not bad, we figured. Twenty cents for three men, and no begging. Mac, too, was averse to begging.

We sliced and toasted half the bread, made a pot of coffee, and fried the salt pork as thin cracklings. With fat from the pork we "buttered" the toast, scrambled six eggs, and fried the potatoes. It was a hearty feed, and we had six boiled eggs and half a loaf of bread saved for the next day. Planning for tomorrow's needs was second nature. Food was important to us, survival imperative.

The next morning, while drinking coffee and eating our bread and boiled eggs, Dave and I decided that being so near Chicago we'd take in the World's Fair and maybe get a job hauling rich or handicapped persons around in rickshaws. Mac suggested that before leaving we might like to take the streetcar across the Mississippi River to St. Paul. That would give him a chance to check the employment situation. If he found nothing, he'd meet us back at the jungle and string along with us down to Chicago. That sounded mighty good. We could use a guide in the world's largest railroad complex.

Dave and I hesitated to spend ten cents each for a pleasure ride, but we followed Mac's suggestion. The trip across Minneapolis, the river, and St. Paul, proved worth the expense. However, at the end of the line we had a surprise: The fare was ten cents in each direction. We could either get off the trolley or pay up again to get back to the jungle. As big spenders we paid up, but we felt profligate all the way back to the jungle.

Upon our return we found Mac. He was disappointed at having had no success finding work in Minneapolis, but eager to try his luck in Chicago. We were sorry for him, but happy to have his further guidance. "Mac," Dave said, "we aren't big-city boys so doubt we can make a go of it in Chicago. After we've seen the World's Fair we'd like to try our luck in the dairy country up Wisconsin way. We'd also kinda like to have a big fat glass of beer in Milwaukee. We might never have another chance to drink real Milwaukee beer in Milwaukee. What do you think?"

"Can't say that I blame you, but times are as tough in dairy country as anywhere else. On the other hand, you might find a chance to work for your grub. That might not be too bad. You could put some fat on your bones eating butter, cream, cheese and such stuff. You could use it. I'll tell you what. We'll take the Soo Line down to Chicago so I can show you where to catch it to Milwaukee. From there you can take the same line on up to Neenah and Menasha, the Twin Cities on Lake Winnebago. Nice towns, especially Neenah." After a moment of thought Mac continued. "It's less than a hundred miles up to Milwaukee, so it's best to ride the blinds on a through passenger train. The blinds are in the space between the engine and the tender. The crew might see you climb aboard, but the Soo is a good road and they shouldn't bother you. I'll show you the ropes when we get to Chicago. Now let's find our way to the Soo Line headed south."

We took time to write a letter to mother, informing her of our plans. We promised to check for mail at the post office in Neenah, Wisconsin. Judging by Mac's account, the Twin Cities area was an attractive destination.

Mac picked his way through the Minneapolis railway yards and found an empty boxcar on a Soo train headed for Chicago. En route he voiced a warning: "You fellows have seen a better class of hobo than you'll find in Chicago. Be on your guard. The guys you've met up with are looking for work. Chicago is a gathering place for all kinds. Some of them are looking for work, but many are riff-raff looking for an easy way to get by. They'll roll you in a minute if they think you've got a dollar. Just hang together, trust nobody, and I mean nobody."

Our boxcar had one flat wheel. With its every revolution the car bounced. The motion was rhythmic, almost hypnotic. Dave stretched out on the floor and soon was fast asleep. His body rose and fell with every cycle. I admired his ability to relax. Mac did too, but he observed: "That's great, but bear in mind that only one of you should sleep. The other one stay alert and keep your back to the wall.

When the train groaned to a stop, Mac picked his way through the labyrinth of the Chicago railway yards, gave us some tips on catching the Milwaukee train, showed us how to get to the fair grounds, and provided some final advice: "Chicago doesn't have a jungle like Minneapolis has, but it has a lot of missions and churches where you can hang out, and soup kitchens where you can get a bite to eat.

"The best place is the Salvation Army. Everybody calls it Sally's. You'll have to get there early, before the place is filled up. You'll get a sermon from a sky pilot, about ten minutes of it, then grub. That'll be a Matthew-Mark-Luke-and-John sandwich. The filling depends on what's surplus at the time. Pay attention to the preacher. He tries to give a good message, and he'll lift your spirits if you listen."

We were sorry to part company with Mac. He had been helpful to us and we hoped that our comradeship had been helpful to him. We followed his directions and found our way to the World's Fair.

# Chapter 13

## Chicago's Brave Facade

Chicago and its Century of Progress: How do a couple of country boys test the waters and get a feel of the place? Chicago, famous as the home of the White Sox and the Cubs; infamous as the headquarters of Al Capone and his gangster henchmen. The Windy City, hub of the country – how do we sense the great throbbing heart that propels it into its second century? How do we distinguish between facade and reality?

Contrary to what we thought, Chicago had not one vast central railroad yard, but many smaller yards spread throughout the city. Fortunately for Dave and me, our Soo Line train pulled into a yard near Lake Shore Drive, only a few blocks west of the 12th Street entrance to the World's Fair.

After craning to see the sights en route, we learned at the entrance booth that admission was fifty cents each. We didn't want to squander a full day's fare for a partial day's fun, so we settled for a copy of the official "Book of the Fair" to study overnight, thus better to gain full value for the cost of admission next day.

An elderly man, strikingly dressed in a scarlet jacket, black trousers with yellow stripes, and a white pith helmet, was lounging near the entrance booth. He was a cop at the fair willing to help a couple of tenderfoots. He made notations on our guidebook on the cost of exhibits. He told us where best to buy the most food for the least cost, and the location of Sally's.

Following his suggestion, we ambled down the waterfront from the Adler Planetarium to 37th Street, taking in the city sights and the fairgrounds across the lagoon. Occasionally our pace quickened as strains of a march by John Philip Sousa rang loud and clear above other festive noises.

Hoping not to miss out on something to eat, Dave and I found our way to the Salvation Army. We especially wished to experience firsthand what mission living was like. The Captain who ushered us into the dining room was impassive but not unkindly. "Be seated for an hour or so," he said.

During the hour or so wait we studied the guidebook. From it we learned that the fair had been planned during the boom years of the 1920's as "A Century of Progress" to display the growth and achievements of the city of Chicago. It was not tax supported. Plans to finance the venture through the sale of bonds failed as the depression worsened. The management decided to build one building, sell the exhibit space, then use the money so raised to put up the next building. They started with the Travel and Transport Building. Before it was up they had enough money from the railroads to put up the next building. Revenues from the sale of exhibit space in that building provided money to construct another building, and so on to completion.

Great help was provided when the "big-three" auto makers – General Motors, Ford, and Chrysler – provided elaborate exhibits at the site. General Motors installed a complete assembly plant. Sears, Roebuck & Company opened a general service pavilion as a goodwill gesture. It housed a hospital, rest rooms, lounge, information booth, and telegraph office. The "big-three" meat-packers – Swift, Armour, and Wilson – set up laboratories and processing plants. At the Wilson pavilion the company dished out tens of thousands of $1.25 steak dinners at a 650-seat roof garden restaurant, and gladly lost money on every one. We decided to by-pass that bargain.

Our attention was diverted from the guidebook to the many men and the few women who had entered the bleak hall while we were reading. The smells of food, barely perceptible when we entered, now permeated the room. Some of the men – we assumed them to be repeat customers – looked longingly at the table which separated the sitting area from the kitchen. They inched forward on their chairs in anticipation of gaining better position in the forthcoming serving line. Serving, however, had to await the formal opening of ceremonies.

A Major of the Salvation Army came forward and introduced a preacher from the church that sponsored the mission. We didn't know what church he represented. We didn't care. To his hushed congregation this sky pilot intoned:

*"Friends, we have seen a violation of God's will. In appearing before you my mission lies not upon the broad highway where tramps the hungry body, but upon the shadowy byway where glides the lonely soul. The message that I bring to you is not for today alone. It is for always.*

*"I feel that within many of you is a sense of waiting, of a want unsatisfied. Your struggle may seem hopeless, but it must be carried on. It must be carried on not today alone, but always. To those souls who seek salvation, I say to you be of good cheer. Repent and follow the teachings of our savior, Jesus Christ. Those who follow the teachings of Jesus will in the end be transported into an orthodox heaven wherein all the harps are kept in tune and all the robes are laundered.*

*"There is no higher heaven. That is my message. May peace be with you. Amen."*

Upon the conclusion of this meaningful prayer, a wizened old man nudged me. "Be blessed that you are fit, my boy. You could say, without a word of a lie, that I never took a backward step in my life until this depression whipped me. Now I'm one of the old fellers that ain't kept too busy. Them in the Bible never had it worse. There just ain't no sense to it all."

We lined up quietly at the table, received our soup, sandwich, and coffee, and ate our meal in silence. While thinking about the sky pilot's message and eating our dinner, Dave and I studied our companions. Most of them were well above middle age. What a shame, we thought, that persons so old could be humbled by circumstance beyond their control.

151

Many of them seemed sad, but none rebellious. The younger participants, apparently hoboes en route from one place to another, were of mixed breed. Some seemed appreciative. Some seemed to accept largess as their due. We vowed to stay away from them.

As the evening progressed we got a surprise. We were not allowed to sleep on the floor, only in our chairs, which were far from comfortable. The lights were turned off at ten o'clock so we could no longer read the guidebook. We survived a night of restless sitting, had breakfast of bread and soup, and concluded that mission life was not for us.

On the way to the fair the next morning we bought a couple of bananas and half a pound of Wisconsin cheese to sustain us until mid-afternoon.

At the entrance booth we paid the admission fees and asked about employment opportunities. The girl said, "We close next Sunday. Your chances are not good but you can go over to the Administration Building and check it out." She pointed out the building to us.

"The season is almost over," she continued. "Jinrikisha jobs are highly competitive among college athletic stars from all over the country. These guys get sixty cents for hauling some dude or duchess around for half an hour. You've gotta be big-time to make money like that. Besides, there's no point in both of you looking for work. Our policy is that only one person in a family can work at the fair. That spreads the employment around. We've got five thousand employees here, and that helps five thousand families."

We accepted her reasoning and set out to enjoy the fair. Dominating the scene were two huge towers half a mile apart. People with money to squander flew through the air on a Sky Ride in rockets suspended on cables two hundred feet above the ground.

Impressive, too, was the 227-foot Great Havoline Thermometer. It was hailed as a "monument to Chicago's climate." We had learned from the guidebook that an even more grandiose display had been deemed impracticable: The

152

construction of a thousand-foot-long papier-mache pickle to advertise the wares of the H.J. Heinz Company.

Having studied the guidebook, Dave and I made good use of our available time. We made a grand reconnaissance of the entire fair to determine where, on following days, we should devote more time. In our survey we satisfied our curiosity about Robert Ripley's "Believe It or Not" exhibit, and Frank Buck's "Bring 'Em Back Alive" jungle camp.

Not least among our ventures was titillating our hitherto subdued sensitivities by ogling Sally Rand in the risque "Streets of Paris" exhibit, where she appeared as Lady Godiva. As she strategically wiggled and undulated her body, she flicked her ostrich-feather fans to the delight of spectators young and old.

Exhausted from the stress of the day's activities, we walked through the Loop, purchased some ready-to-eat groceries and a brown cloth bag to carry the many brochures we had collected throughout the day. We took the Douglas Park transit line from the center of the city as far as our fares would carry us.

A few blocks beyond the end of the transit line we observed a piano box in the yard of a modest house. In answer to our knock a young man appeared, followed by a couple of youngsters. "Sir," Dave said, "we came to Chicago to see the fair, but we don't like to be in the city at night. We hope you won't mind if we sleep in your piano box for a night or two. We'd like to get out of the weather, and we won't be a bit of trouble to you."

The man came outside to look us over. After a moment he called his wife. "Hon," he said, "these fellows want to sleep in your piano box for a couple of nights. They look all right to me. What do you think?"

She gave tentative approval: "I'm saving it to make a rabbit hutch. As long as you don't disturb it, I don't have any objections. It's okay with me."

It was okay for Dave and me, too. We settled in for a good night's sleep. The next morning we retraced our course and spent the entire day at the fair. Our special focus was on the General Motors assembly plant, the Great Hall of Science where we had to stand ten deep to study the geological time clock exhibit, and the Transport Building where we studied the layout of the zone between a locomotive and its tender. Our railroader friend Mac had suggested that we use this zone, called the blinds, on our forthcoming journey to Milwaukee. Of interest, too, was a novel invention just introduced. It was called air conditioning.

We could have moved on to Milwaukee, but that morning we had left our bag and belongings with our host. We returned to the piano box and en route bought a couple of toy rabbits for the youngsters. Their mother was pleased at our thoughtfulness. She gave us hot coffee to wash down our bread and liverwurst.

While munching our food we planned the next day's activities. "We've had a pretty good look at the Fair but we haven't seen the real Chicago," Dave said. "As long as we're here let's see what makes the place tick before we head for Milwaukee." That sounded good to me.

Next morning, with our belongings and brochures tucked in our bag, we took the train to the city and took off to see the sights in the downtown Loop area. The Palmer House Hotel and the Sears Roebuck, Marshall Field, and Charles A. Stevens stores were impressive indeed.

However, we hadn't come to be impressed. We wanted to see the other side of life. We found it while sauntering along West Madison Street, and in Washington Park between 51st and 61st Streets.

Dressed in our travel garb we felt more at ease on Skid Row than on the more prosperous streets of the city. But we were soon distressed at seeing this mecca, this degrading substitute for a hobo jungle. Tramps and bums, huddled in doorways or sleeping in alleys, provided stark contrast to hoboes living in the privacy of a jungle. Winos begging for money and pimps soliciting business for their "fancy ladies" vied for our attention.

"Dave," I said, "I've heard how aggressively vendors peddle their wares in Calcutta, but I think they couldn't compete with these winos and pimps."

"You're right," Dave replied, "I think that too, but one thing for sure: I wouldn't trade one of those cigarette girls at the fair for all the whores in this city."

Tattoo parlors displayed in gaudy colors the artistry of the craft: The American flag, a serpent crawling round and round a muscular forearm, or a fetching rendition of a pinup girl. This pinup girl, the sign announced, could emphasize either the big bosom, the long legs, the scant attire, or all three. "We give the customer what he wants," proclaimed the sign.

Frequently several businesses occupied the same structure. At street level on one side of the entrance might be a burlesque house that advertised "Come right in – ten cents a show." On the other side might be a medicine faker who advertised "Medicines – We Cure All Ailments." A sign above the doorway might advertise "Rooms Upstairs – 25 cents." From the entrance to the saloon across the street one could see in many of the rooms a red light glowing, the signal that a hooker was available in this fancy house.

An elderly man selling apples on a street corner at five cents each saw that we were newcomers. He wanted to talk and found in us a receptive audience. "So you boys think this is rough country, do you? Well you ain't seen nothing yet. You ain't seen nothing compared to Cicero. In this part of the city we've got a saloon or two on every block. In Cicero every other joint's a saloon mixed up with a gamblin' den and a whorehouse. Al Capone owns 'em all. He owns that whole damn town. If you wanta see life in the raw go see Cicero, but I wouldn't recommend it."

We didn't go to Cicero. Content in knowing that we "ain't seen nothing yet," we had seen enough; we caught a train and rode the blinds to Milwaukee. En route to the Soo yards we thought about the World's Fair and the disparity between the facade it presented and the reality of the city that nurtured it.

Although construction of the World's Fair was launched during the early stage of the Great Depresion, the committee and its managers persevered. They proclaimed, "Recessions are as temporary as the cloud that momentarily obscures the sun."

They touted "Victories of a glorious past and the Promise of a more glorious future." They announced a "Beacon in the darkness of the depression."

The World's Fair truly became a beacon in the darkness. As evidence of confidence in the future and of hope for better times, it gave a welcome psychological lift to the millions who came to enjoy the endless opportunities for interest and wonder. It took a lot of people's minds off the Great Depression. However, it provided scant solace to many. Better times were a long way in the future. The World's Fair was the facade of prosperity. Chicago was the reality of adversity.

# Chapter 14

# Journey's End

As our friend Mac had informed us, an advantage of riding the blinds on a passenger train was that it brought us directly into the center of town. We piled off in the heart of Milwaukee. Now we'd have a glass of that famous Milwaukee beer. We entered a tavern and ordered a couple of beers.

"What size?"

"Big ones."

"That'll be fifteen cents straight, or two for a quarter," said the bartender. He drew two 16-ounce mugs of draft beer and deftly swirled off the heads of foam as he slid them across the bar.

Having anticipated this luxury for so long, we downed our beers with gusto. At a cost of only two for a quarter, we figured we'd have seconds. We did. After a bit the bartender meandered back and served us two more. "The third round is on the house," he said. "Besides, we're happy to see the end of prohibition and the coppersmiths back to work at the breweries again. We can afford to be generous." He was a friendly guy.

When we stood up to leave we were tipsy. "My God, that's not three point two beer," I said. "It must be six percent alcohol. Dave, let's sit down for a minute and get our bearings."

"Ha ha, buddy, you're right," the bartender said. "That's six percent beer and it'll make a man outta ya. Just relax for a few minutes and you'll be okay."

This is not the kind of beer that I used to make, I mused, as the wooziness continued and my thoughts raced backward in time. My next older brother Marlin and I had a bright idea when we were kids in Silver City. We'd make home brew in our cabin and peddle it at dances and ball games at two-bits for a twelve-ounce "pint" bottle. We did things in a big way. We brewed our beer in a fifty gallon barrel. To maintain proper brewing temperature we submerged a hundred-watt lamp, carefully taped into the socket to eliminate electrical shorts, near the bottom of the barrel. The local baker provided malt, hops, yeast, and sugar in exchange for all the beer he could drink. We gathered beer bottles at the town dump. Our only expense was for bottle caps and gasoline for our delivery jalopy. We developed a thriving and profitable business until our father got wind of it. He was, it seemed at the time, a problem.

As my reverie drew to a close the wooziness abated. Dave and I left the tavern to take in the town. It was a big town and there was much to see. As we wandered the streets our brown bag, stuffed with brochures from the world's fair, got heavier and heavier. Dave took one handle of the bag and I the other. As we were walking along the sidewalk, a patrol car pulled alongside. Two cops were in the front seat. Two sawed-off shotguns hung on the fence barrier that separated the front from the rear seat.

"Whatcha mugs got in that bag?" one of them barked.

"Just our bindles and some brochures from the Chicago fair."

"Give us a look, and no funny business."

We moved to open the door and pass him the bag.

"Goddamn it, give me the bag through the window."

Apparently some sort of "funny business" could be perpetrated through the door of the car but not through the window. We passed the bag through the window. They pawed through it.

"We don't want no goddamn bums here. D'ya see that road? Take it and get the hell outta town quick."

We saw that road. We got the hell outta town quick. Cops with Al Capone-type manner were not to our liking. We got to Neenah as fast as the first northbound freight train would get us there.

*   *   *   *

Our first exposure to Neenah was a pleasant one. A hand lettered sign in the window of a corner grocery store announced "Milk – five cents for the first quart. Four cents for each additional quart." We bought two quarts, laid nine cents on the counter, and started to leave.

"Hey, there's a penny apiece deposit on them bottles."

"Never mind, we'll just drink 'em around the corner and bring back the empties."

With as much gusto as drinking Milwaukee beer, we consumed the milk. When we returned the bottles the grocer directed us to the post office. There was no mail addressed to us. We assured the clerk that mail was forthcoming and we would be back in a few days. We asked him to hold it for us.

We meandered about town and on the outskirts found a dairy farmer who could use us for a few days. We made ourselves useful in general. Dave did so in particular, cutting the hair of the farmer and all his children.

After a few days a letter arrived from our mother. President Roosevelt had increased the price of gold to $35 per ounce. As a result, Pappy had developed gold fever. He had explored some old mine workings and found where he could make some money at that price if he had some help. "Wouldn't you like to join him in this venture?"

Not that her letter was a request; not that a spot of smudged ink on the paper was evidence of a tear dropped in the writing. No, a lifetime bond of understanding made evident her yearning for us to come home. Her letter was like the first flowering of a bud on a barren landscape.

The longest part of a journey is said to be the passing of the gate. We had passed that gate when we departed Salt Lake City on Independence Day. What had the journey accomplished? It had removed from our destitute family the responsibility for our keep. It had provided for us experience that we would never forget, but that we would never choose to repeat. Shall we abort that journey, not yet fulfilled? Yes, we'll abort the journey, but we'll continue the search.

"Mother," we wrote, "maybe this is the chance we've been looking for. Of course we'll return. We'll hop the first freight train west and be home pretty quick. Don't worry about us. We know the ropes."

When we said good-bye to the farmer, he slipped us a dollar apiece. This was a pleasant surprise. We hadn't expected any pay. Those two dollars doubled our reserve. We could get home now with money to spare. Nobody likes to go home dead broke.

We struck out for the Soo Railroad yards, and were fortunate to find an agent who took time to help us work out the best route home. "Well, boys," he said, "I know my own territory pretty good, but to get out west we'd better check the Official Railway Guide. You could either go to Chicago and then hit the Union Pacific due west, or you could go to Minneapolis-St. Paul, and start from there."

"We've had enough of Chicago. How do we get to Salt Lake from Minneapolis?"

"You've got to go both south and west. From Minnie you can go south to Omaha then west, or you can go west to Butte and then south."

"We've had enough of Butte. How do we get from Minnie to Salt Lake by way of Omaha?"

"Well, I'll tell you the best way to go. You take this here Soo Line to Minnie. Then you take the Chicago & Northwestern to Marshalltown, Iowa. That's maybe 350 miles. Then on to Omaha for another hundred plus. From there you take the Union Pacific all the way. You'll go through Grand Island, North Platte, Julesburg, Cheyenne, Granger, and Ogden. When you get that far you're home free."

We thanked this kindly man for his advice. We managed to arrive at the Minnie jungle, the first leg of our homeward trip, before dark. Our interest was aroused by a group of transients lolling around, listening to someone giving a speech. Idle curiosity whetted our interest and we drew near. We didn't have to mingle long to sense that there was something more than idle curiosity that drew together this gathering of destitute men. We edged closer and found that the speaker was a Prairie Preacher.

160

Why do men congregate to hear the words of a self-proclaimed Man of God, we wondered. Our conclusion was that, as flies gather where the sugar is, so do men who have lost their faith hunger for something to restore their hope. Believing in nothing, but wanting to believe in something, they embrace whatever might restore their self esteem.

Some persons can carry the faith better than others. This Prairie Preacher was a master at getting his listeners to join him in dialogue. "The lonely can communicate their sadness," he was saying, "but they have great difficulty in overcoming it. Is anyone lonely?"

"Yes, I'm lonely," one listener responded. "In tough times women are stronger than men. Anyway, my wife is stronger than me. We had just enough to keep from starving. I couldn't take it no more, so I pulled stakes. But I can't take this, either, so I'm going back home. I'm lonesome for the bad old days."

"Good for you, brother," the preacher said. "When you get down so low that you can't get any lower, there's no place to go but up. You lie down to die or you pull yourself up and start over, like you're doing. Anyone else?"

"Yes," another one said. "I left home, too. Before I left I hammered pork-and-beans cans flat and nailed 'em over the holes where the rats come in. My wife wouldn't come with me so I left her home wearing her flour-sack fashions. Me? This depression has made me live the law of the jungle. I jungle up, then bum the town. Sometimes I find a garbage can bonanza. Sometimes I find rat poison in the trash can. But no more gopher pie for me. I'll take my chances on the road."

"My friend," the preacher said, "hard times are for the poor, but the idea that it's criminal to be poor is not true. Dishonesty sometimes is just another word for survival. Starvation? It depends on what you had before. Nobody listens to reason on an empty stomach. I say to you, fill your stomach as a poor man, but not as a criminal."

Another man, of the type known on the road as an Elegant Bum, spoke up. "Preacher, if I can hustle a living without working, I'm not beating another fellow out of a job. If I do an honest hustle, isn't that all right? Let's say I work a week and get a paycheck. While the other workers are feeling flush with a week's wages in hand, I raffle my paycheck to 'em at a dollar a crack, and end up with the equal of two or three paychecks. Everybody who buys a ticket has an equal chance and nobody is much of a loser. So don't you figure I'm a good hustler, to quit my job so someone else can find work?"

While the preacher was pondering a response to that question, Dave and I sought out a place in the jungle that offered privacy. We took a bath and were boiling our clothes when a stranger approached. On the road you don't approach another man's campfire unless invited. This fellow had something on his mind. He was a large man of indeterminate age, perhaps in his mid-forties. He came right to the point.

"You fellers goin' west? Maybe you can help me out."

"Yes, we're going west. What's your problem?"

"Well, it ain't my problem, but I feel kinda responsible for this family. I've nursemaided 'em this far but I'm takin' a branch line to Kansas City and I'm feared for 'em. This guy's takin' his wife and kid out to Oregon and he don't know nothing. Maybe you could string along with 'em and they won't get rolled. They're carryin' their life savin's with 'em. It don't amount to much, but it's all they've got."

"How come you take an interest in them?"

"It's like this: I see a coupla punks in the Chicago yard lookin' over this family of tenderfeet and their great big bundles, so I figure I'll keep an eye out. Sure as hell, when the guy leaves his wife and daughter to get some grub these young punks grab two of the bundles and strike out. I take after 'em, and when they see I'm bigger'n both of 'em they drop the bundles. When I lug 'em back I see these folks really need somebody to look after 'em. I shoulda gone direct to Kansas City, but I figure it won't do me no harm to take a detour and help 'em as far as Marshalltown. Maybe you fellers can help 'em a little farther?"

"Let's go over and have a talk with them," Dave suggested We didn't have much chance to talk. The three of them were so effusive in thanking their benefactor for his help, and expressing

162

sorrow at his departure, that we found no opening for questions. Nor did we have need for questions. This man was clearly motivated only by caring for others. The others clearly needed help along the way. We offered our help.

"My name's Joseph Wilson. My friends call me Joe," the man said. "This is Flora, and the girl is Julie. We won't be a burden and we can pay for our keep. We've got some donuts and cheese we can share with you."

"Let's save that for dessert," I said. "First have some stew that we're cooking up."

We lugged their three bundles to our campsite. They were large bundles and they were heavy. Flora half apologized and half explained, "When we left home we knew it was forever. So we took our prized possessions and we couldn't shrink down any more. We simply couldn't."

Joseph Wilson and his family were not a burden, but their bundles were. They were so heavy we couldn't board a moving train. We had to pile on while it was stopped. Fortunately, railroad men looked the other way when they observed the women in our group. Other hoboes on the road granted us privacy. The Wilsons were not private persons. Their life history came gushing forth.

"Life isn't fair," Flora said. "I lost my husband, and with Julie to look after I took a job teaching. Joe was a bachelor and he was teaching in the same school. We developed a fond attachment and after a few years got married. What happened next? I lost my job because I was now married. The School Board didn't want to let me go, but that was the law. They had to spread the work around. If a woman was married, her husband was the provider. It just isn't fair."

Joe broke in. "We could have got married on the sly and lived in sin, but that wasn't our way. Besides, we were both so well regarded in the school we thought they would make an exception. But they didn't. We can't live on my salary, and Flora loves to teach. So we're going out to a remote part of Oregon where they have so much trouble getting teachers that to

163

get one of us they might take two of us, even though we're married."

"That makes sense," Dave said. "We'll string along together as far as Granger, Wyoming. From there you'll take the northern branch through Idaho into Oregon. That's a major line of the Union Pacific and you should stay right with it. We'll get you headed in the right direction and help you climb aboard."

As we rode a boxcar south from Marshalltown, and another one west out of Omaha, the Wilsons expressed wonder at the variety of life and scenery as seen from the railroad tracks. "This is some different from the so-called industrial heartland of South Chicago," Joe said. "We saw miles of abandoned factories with boarded up windows and idle smokestacks. The parking lots were grown up with weeds. On both sides of the track was evidence of choices made, then discarded -- deserted automobiles, scattered tires, rusted appliances, junk, junk, junk."

"But even worse is the plight of the people," Flora said. "The train ran through block after block of ghetto housing where families sat together on makeshift porches. They paid no attention to our passing train. Instead, they stared at the trash heap that littered the dooryard, waiting for God knows what. Here on the Nebraska prairie, where the world is so big, the Great Depression has hit hard, but the people are so spread out they can hide their private kind of shame."

Comments by our traveling companions opened wider my own view of this vast country. Trains skim impassively across the landscape. All of life is there to see beside the rails: the cities and towns, the farms and prairies, and the people who in times of national catastrophe live out their lives in quiet desperation.

The slums of the cities reflect hopelessness born of human degradation. Despair fades as the freight train lumbers into the verdant countryside, where signs of a prosperous past give hope for the future. Despair and hope intermingle as the cycle begins again and dilapidated buildings dominate the scene.

The Wilson family was making a desperate attempt to better their lot in life. Dave and I guided them safely as far as Granger, and got them settled in a boxcar headed for Oregon. Feeling that it was a job well done, we made our way to Salt Lake City.

"My goodness, boys, I'm glad to see you, but you look like scarecrows," our mother said when we got home. "I'll fix something to eat while you clean up." I had shrunk from 165 to 138 pounds. After eating only a portion of her substantial meal we were stuffed. That evening we ate larger portions. The next few days she couldn't fill us up. As our systems became accustomed to larger quantities of food, our innards swelled back to normal and so did our weight. We were eager to get to work.

# PART 3

# ENTREPRENEURS

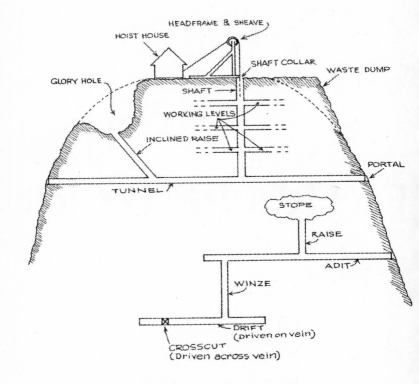

**Nomenclature of mine workings**

# Chapter 15

# Gold Fever

As boys we had called our father "Pappy." We returned from our journey as his partners. We now called him "Super," a title that pleased him. When Super returned from "scouting the mines" he outlined his plans.

"The smelter at Garfield," he began, "has reduced its smelting charge for siliceous ores from the Tintic District. It wants quartz-based ores to flux with the sulfide ores coming out of Bingham Canyon, so it can smelt at a lower temperature. It's worked out a deal with the railroad to reduce shipping charges. With the price of gold and silver up, and the cost of smelting and freight down, we ought to be able to make a dollar.

"I've just signed a lease with the North Lily Mining Company, the outfit that manages the abandoned mines above Silver City. Big companies can't make a go of scavenging old mine workings, so their best bet is to lease them out to little fellows like us. They do all the book work and hold back royalty, which depends on the value of the ore. Our success is their success, so they'll help us out. It's a good deal if we can find the ore.

"I've found a pocket of ore that'll get us started. It's at the old Carissa mine where the orebody was mined out so close to the surface that the roof caved in and left a big glory hole. The pocket of ore they missed is now accessible from the surface. I figure it'll run about sixty tons, and my samples assayed about twelve dollars to the ton.

"All we've got to do is buy a little blasting powder, mine it out, and haul it to the tipple at Eureka. We can use the old Kissel truck for that. Our deductions will total less than five dollars a ton.  Assuming sixty tons, we'll clean up more than four hundred dollars. That's more money than we've seen in a year. What do you think?"

We knew that it's bad enough for an entrepreneur to develop a fever, but to be smitten by gold fever is unmitigated catastrophe—at once the most exciting and the least containable malady to disrupt the thinking process. Dave sensed that Super had been smitten, and would have no peace of mind until he

**Kissel truck, year 1914. Upper photo, used by Super as a school bus on an earlier venture. Lower sketch, as adapted to haul ore from the Little Spy Mine to the railroad tipple**

struck it rich. "There's the rub," he said. "Where's the ore? I'd be a millionaire if I just knew where to dig. It might take a long time to find out what's in that hole in the ground. What you say sounds pretty good, but after we've stripped the Carissa glory hole, where do we go from there?"

"That depends on how smart we are," Super replied. "After we strip the Carissa, winter will be on us. I figure if we spend our time scouting the old mines we'll find something to keep us going."

Dave's eyes met mine. Shall we back Super's hunch? I nodded. He said, "Let's get on with it."

We stuffed our gear into the rumble seat of our 1930 Ford Model-A roadster and headed for the Carissa glory hole in the Tintic Mining District. Super was a good blacksmith. He sharpened some drill steel. While Dave and I single-jacked holes and blasted the ore free, Super rigged a windlass to hoist it to the surface. We hauled the ore to the transfer tipple at Eureka in the Kissel truck that Super had used on a previous venture. He had bought it in 1914 to transport school children from the outlying communities to the central high school in Eureka. It could be adapted to this job.

While waiting for the settlement returns on our ore shipment, we dug in for the winter. On the dump of the Northern Spy mine we built a plank floor and mounted a twelve-by-twelve foot army tent with sideboards four feet high. Furnished with a cot, a double bed, a sheet-metal stove, and a table and benches, this was a cozy camp. It was all we needed for shelter.

Our tent was shelter, also, for two uninvited guests. Soon after we extinguished our Coleman lantern, the sound of pitter-patter on the plank floor roused us. Super switched on his flashlight and we saw two little skunks in the woodbox, exploring the contents, especially the waxed bread wrappings. I picked up a shoe to throw at them. Super barked, "Whoa, Cy, if you scare 'em they'll fumigate us out of here for a month. Just leave 'em alone, and we'll see what happens."

The skunks investigated the woodbox to their satisfaction, sniffed around a bit, and settled down for the night under the sheet-metal stove. When our alarm clock sounded in the morning, the skunks strolled out of the tent as casually as they had come in. "They only wanted to get out of the cold," Super observed.

That night, before retiring, he placed some food scraps in the woodbox, and an old army blanket under the stove. The skunks arrived soon after the light went out. They apparently enjoyed their welcome, as they joined us every night that cold weather continued. We enjoyed the company of two nice little pets.

When the settlement on the ore shipment arrived we were elated. There must have been hidden veinlets of highgrade gold and silver that Super's samples didn't catch. The ore value was not twelve but thirty dollars per ton. Our check was for more than eleven hundred dollars. That covered all our bills and left money to spare for further ventures.

Throughout the winter of 1934 Super, Dave, and I explored mines that had been abandoned in the silver panic of 1897. We were seeking deposits which when explored were considered waste, but at the increased price of gold might be profitable ore. It was an arduous and sometimes dangerous search.

The Northern Spy was remembered by old-timers as a mine that contained vast deposits but of low grade. It had been developed by sinking a shaft to a depth of nine hundred feet. At hundred-foot intervals roomy stations had been excavated. From these stations drifts had been run along the metalliferous zone.

Surrounding the shaft at the surface was a large waste dump. From it we took samples of scattered pieces of quartz and barite – the minerals associated with vein formation in the area. Assay results from our samples were encouraging. We decided this mine was worth exploring.

Problems in exploring the Northern Spy were formidable. The hoist house had disintegrated, and the headframe had collapsed. The collar of the shaft was a mere depression in the hillside. It was covered with debris which left only a few peep-holes from which we could see down the shaft. Other access to the mine had to be found. We found it through the Little Spy, a mine several hundred yards to the north and somewhat lower in elevation.

The Little Spy had an inclined shaft which bottomed at 128 feet. From there we could inch our way along drifts and open stopes to reach the station at the 300-foot level of the Northern Spy. Super figured out how we could get from that station down to the lower levels.

"Do you see those deep hitches cut into the far side of the shaft?" he asked. "They were cut out for the original shaft timbering. We'll snake over a couple of 4 x 4 inch timbers and rest one end of each timber in hitches, and the other ends here on the station where we'll mount a windlass. We'll anchor a support across the 4 x 4s near the center of the shaft and swing a pulley from it. With two men on the windlass and a strong rope from it through the pulley, the third man can be lowered pretty slick."

**Windlass installed on the 300-foot level of the Northern Spy Mine**

We went to work on that basis -- cautiously. When construction was complete, Super insisted that he go first, that we lower him down to the 400-foot level to test our work. He loaded himself down with a prospector's pick, sample sacks, and extra carbide for his lamp. He inched himself along the 4 x 4s

173

and straddled a pick handle that he tied to the end of the windlass rope. He wound a cord around his body and the rope. "If I get knocked out from falling debris I don't want to fall off this bosun's chair," he said, and rang two bells.

We were concerned that any loud noise might reverberate and dislodge timbers hanging in the shaft, so we provided a muted bell with a separate bell cord. One bell meant "stop" if in motion, and "raise" if not. Two bells meant "lower," three meant "man aboard."

Dave and I lowered Super carefully, very carefully, until we heard the bell ring once. We could see the rope swinging back and forth. The motion slowed to a stop. The bell rang ding-ding. We lowered the rope slightly, ever so slightly, until the bell rang one ding. The rope moved back and forth again, then came to a stop. We knew that Super had swayed as a pendulum until he could jump to sure footing on the station of the 400-foot level.

After what seemed like hours of anxious waiting, we heard three bells, the "man aboard" signal, and after a pause, a single bell. We cranked the windlass, and raised Super and his samples to the 300-foot station of the Northern Spy. We wiggled our way back to the shaft of the Little Spy, thence to the surface and our tent. The ore samples looked promising. We would go back for more.

Super, having led the way and satisfied himself that our rigging was sound, allowed his boys to explore the rest of the mine. The next day Dave took his turn, and explored the 500-foot level. He took a lunch to make a day of it, and a gunny sack so he could send a large number of samples to our working level in advance of being hoisted himself.

That evening we made plans to explore the 500-foot level, then examine our samples and select the most promising ones to be assayed. On the basis of test results. we would determine our future course of action. We would not explore deeper than the 600-foot level, which was near the end of our rope. Further, none of us relished exposure to the hazards involved if the prize at the end seemed unworthy.

"Cy," Super said next morning, "the deeper we go, the harder it'll be to sway back and forth to get to the station. I'll fashion a fork on the end of a long pole so you can push against the opposite side of the shaft. Then you won't have to swing like a pendulum. I'll put an outboard hook on the fork so when you're ready to come up you can use it to pull the rope from the shaft over to you at the station."

With the pole added to my other gear, I straddled the pick handle, super's "bosun's chair," and said, "Let her rip," in the calmest voice I could muster. Super and Dave lowered me until I rang the bell at the 600-foot level. The forked pole was handy in pushing me over from the shaft to the station.

The mineralized zone on the 600-foot level was similar to that observed by Dave and Super on the upper levels. The gangue material was honeycomb quartz, a dirty white about the color of our laundry, with patches of barite here and there. The drift had been driven in both directions several hundred feet, to the ends of the property I assumed.

I took samples at promising places along the deposit, labeled them, and marked the sites with soot by playing the flame of my carbide lamp on the spots selected. As I took one sample, I rose from a stooped position and my head hit a protruding rock. The lamp flew off my miner's cap and the flame went out. The world was black as coal and I had lost my only source of light. In panic, I pawed the area where I thought it had fallen. It was not there. I sniffed here and there but sensed not a whiff of my carbide lamp. My God, I thought, what do I do now? I can search in one direction, then the other, but how can I know when I'm back where I lost the lamp? If I don't find it, how do I find my way to the shaft?

In naked fear I started to quiver and tremble, then came to my senses, sat down, and recovered my wits. I knew the relationship of the shaft to where I was, but I might become confused in searching back and forth. So I laid my cap on the middle of the drift with the visor pointed in the direction of the shaft, and searched for my lamp in both directions. When I didn't find it, I did next best and felt my way toward the shaft.

By and by, I heard the distinctive sound of bats. Aha, I thought, this might be a good omen, like the sight of birds by a seaman long adrift. I searched with renewed vigor, and suddenly stumbled on something familiar. It was the pole Super had made, lying on the station where I had left it. What a godsend, I thought. Maybe I'll make it.

With the pole I probed the wall in all directions. Where it opened wide, there was the shaft. I crawled toward the edge and waved the pole back and forth until it touched the rope. I pulled the pole back into the station. The rope was caught in the hook. With trembling hands I grasped it and the pick handle bosun's seat.

To assure myself that Super and Dave were manning the windlass, and to alert them that I would soon be on board, I rang two bells to lower the rope, and one bell to stop. I then rang three bells, straddled the pick handle, inched myself to the middle of the shaft by using the forked pole, and rang one bell to be hoisted to the 300-foot level and safety.

When I finished telling my story, Dave said, "I'll go down and get the samples and your lamp."

"The hell with it," I murmured, "let's call it a day."

From among our many samples we selected a few and took them to the assay office. Upon analyzing the results we concluded that the Northern Spy could be mined profitably only on a large scale, that we didn't have the resources to develop it, and that our hazardous exploration had been for naught. We would have to look elsewhere for a profitable venture. We had barely accepted these sad facts when distress of a different sort developed.

\*    \*    \*    \*

We had an adequate reserve of basic foodstuffs, but had to go to Eureka every week or so for fresh produce. When heavy snows made driving impossible we walked to town, following the upper track of the narrow, winding roadway. The trail we made was the only evidence that a road existed on the steep hillside.

One night Super started to moan and groan. He was a stoic, so Dave and I knew something was seriously wrong. He was shaking violently with chills. We made a roaring fire. His temperature soared. He changed back and forth between chills and fever. We held a board of directors meeting and decided we had to get him to a doctor. Quick. It was then three o'clock in the morning. Dave's plan was simple: "You strike out for Eureka and find a team of horses to pull us out of here. I'll shovel the roadway so when you return the team can pull the car back and forth to get it started."

I hiked to town and found a man in his stable tending horses. He had been alerted to use his sled to deliver groceries for P.J. Fennel & Company because of the heavy snows. He said, "Have you got a chain?"

"Yes."

He anchored a double-tree to the hames of one harness and a single-trees to the other. "Pile on," he said.

We rode the horses single file on the upper track of the roadway. Upon arriving at the tent we found Dave cutting a hole in the floorboard of our Ford roadster. It had no heater, but it had a "cut-out" directly back of the exhaust manifold. This was a specialty feature of sporty cars for sporty drivers.It allowed the exhaust to roar out of the cut-out opening rather than pass through the muffler. Dave cut the hole in the floorboard so the hot exhaust gases would come full force into the car, an effective but hazardous heater.

While I kept the tent warm and tended to Super, Dave and the teamster managed to start the car by towing it back and forth with the team. They revved it up until it was steamy hot. We got Super into the car, covered him with blankets and coats, and drove to town. We were surprised and pleased to arrive at Eureka without serious incident.

"Much obliged," we said to the teamster. "What's the charge?"

"Not a thing. Old Pat Fennel won't know the difference."

After his terrible night of agony, Super seemed to be feeling better. The farther we drove the better he felt. When we arrived home in Salt Lake City he didn't want to see a doctor, and that was that. Mother didn't argue. She just used her natural smarts and the next time an attack struck, our family doctor was primed for the occasion.

"David," the doctor said on the telephone, "I can't see you till this afternoon, and when I do see you I want to make some tests that I can't perform in the office. I'll make the arrangements and you go over to the Holy Cross Hospital. I'll see you about five o'clock." John J. Galligan was a competent and a persuasive doctor. Super went to the hospital so the doctor could perform "some tests."

The next morning Super awoke and said to mother at bedside, "Gee, that was a good sleep and a good rest. When the Doc said he was going to relax me with a little shot in the back I didn't realize I'd sleep all night." He moved about a bit and felt the bandages at his midsection. "My God, Jessie, what happened to me?" he asked.

"Not much. The doctor just took out your appendix. Now you won't have trouble like that again."

Super had no more trouble, and we were able to start searching elsewhere for a profitable venture. That elsewhere was most likely the Little Spy mine. Having used its underground workings as passageway to the Northern Spy, we were familiar with the mine and impressed by some of the large open stopes that had been mined out. Random samples assayed richer than those from the Northern Spy. "We've been blind to a good little thing that doesn't require too much development work, Super said, "while we've been looking for a good big thing that we couldn't handle if we found it. We can make the Little Spy pay if we can work on a fairly large scale. Lets take a hard look and figure out what we have to do. Then we'll tackle the jobs one by one."

The Little Spy hadn't been worked since 1897. The shaft had been sunk along the vein at an incline of about fifteen degrees from the vertical. The original buildings had collapsed. Only the headframe remained, and that was tilted because of decay at both the bottom of the 12 x 12 inch upright timbers and the sills on which they were mounted. A horse whim had been used as a hoist, judging from the trodden path that circled around the shaft.

"Let's do first things first," Super said. "I'll get a modern hoist and an air compressor, and build a shed around them while you fellows straighten up the headframe and build an ore bin."

Super borrowed a pneumatic hoist and purchased an air compressor. He powered it with the Peerless V-8 automobile engine salvaged from his railroading venture. Dave and I sawed a couple of feet off the posts of the headframe to get rid of the dry rot, replaced the sills under them, and built a bin that would hold two carloads of ore. We helped Super install the hoist and compressor in the shed, and were ready to tackle the underground work.

"When I arranged to borrow the hoist from the North Lily mine," Super said, "the boss said he had a skip we might find useful on an inclined shaft. That'll be better than hoisting with a bucket, but we'll have to install rails down the shaft to use it."

We installed the rails, borrowed the skip, and retimbered the chute and ore bin at the bottom of the shaft so we could use them. We installed an air line from the compressor to the orebody, assembled Jackhammers from parts scrounged at abandoned mine repair shops, lowered a minecar to the working level, and laid rails from the stope to the underground bin.

The old-timers used wheelbarrows, called Irish buggies, instead of minecars. In cleaning up the drift to lay the rails, we found that the rock we removed could be shipped at a profit. In the vernacular, it was "pay dirt."

By the time the road was clear of snow we were ready to ship. With Super manning the hoist and tending the compressor, Dave and I mined and shipped a carload of ore each week. When the settlement sheets arrived, with payments of four to six hundred dollars for each carload, we were jubilant. We had lived dangerously on scant fare to develop the Little Spy to the production stage. We were ready to reap the reward.

"We're making a good start," Super said one evening. "We'll make some real money when the other boys get here and fill out the crew. Dick will graduate from high school in June and Marlin will finish his hitch in the Navy soon after. We'd better make some changes."

"The best thing we can do," Dave suggested, "is to fix up some more bunk space. The tent has served the three of us pretty well, but with extra men we'll need more room."

An abandoned building stood not far from the Little Spy. It appeared to have been a combination boarding and rooming house for an adjoining mine. We appropriated this old house, and renovated it to accommodate our full crew, with a special room for mother, who was an essential cog in the entrepreneurial enterprise.

Ours was a man's world, dominated by a man's view of that world. There was another view, however, and that was mother's. It was not dissimilar but more sensitive and focused on the finer things of life. After visiting us at the mine on one occasion she expressed that view in what she called "Some hastily composed verses," which follow.

### Vacation at the Mine

Summer time, vacation time, the house is empty quite;
Husband and sons are at the mine. They've made a gallant fight
To conquer unemployment, to keep family budget straight.
No simple thing these doleful days, to keep a home and eight.

"Now, mother, you stay home and rest, the mine's no place for you;
We'll mine the ore, we'll haul the stuff, we'll do our cooking too.
We have a shanty in the hills, our appetites are fine,
So now good-bye." and they were off, all seven, to the mine.

Now the city is no place to spend the glorious summertime.
And home has never given me, much time that's really mine.
So I shall climb the mountains, too, and see my men at work.
I'll invade their man's dominion, I'll not read or dream and shirk.

180

So I am off. The city, then the farms are left behind;
We twist and climb, the car holds to the road with crunch and grind.
The short turns make one clutch and gasp, great chasms yawn below,
The air is thin; I see beyond for twenty miles I know.

A last sharp curve and there's the mine, tucked right in the hill.
(Man, impudent, irreverent, bends Nature to his will).
A grimy man with squinting face is clutching the controls,
My husband's eyes smile out at me; a huge cable unrolls.

Great wheels are turning; wooden frame is trembling with the strain.
A skip is hoisted up the shaft, is dumped and down again;
The car of ore is trundled off and tripped into a bin.
That lad in ore-stained clothes, I see our high school boy in him.

A big truck rumbles in, is steered in place without delay,
The ore released, now tumbles through; the box is filled that way.
The truck driver is off again, his hair wild in the breeze,
He turns his head, a smile reveals our sailor boy is pleased.

A bell rings out, another signal from the men below,
Those hard-rock miners down the shaft are our college boys you know.
But as the whistle shrieks for noon, they climb out one by one,
With splattered faces, tired eyes, glad dinner hour has come.

Our youngest son is at the shack, with table set to dine,
Camp dishes laid in boyish style, the kettle boiling fine.
We make the coffee, find some fruit, and cook great piles of meat;
Rough benches placed -- these men of mine can hardly wait to eat.

I look about; this grimy room with clutter everywhere,
Has just become important. for my boys find comfort there.
Work rugged, elemental, could there be more sane appeal
For a nobler and a fuller life? Camp life is cruel but real.

When muscle, brain, tool and machine, co-ordinate as one

The task performed is greater far, than wages which are won;
Each individual knows full well how much depends on him,
It's all for each and each for all, no slave, so boss so grim.
Too well I know what risks are run in those awful sunless vaults,
From such chill and clammy caverns, our light-loving souls revolt.
But the world would be insipid, dull, a place for craven souls,
If no one dared to risk his life in work for higher goals.

And neither can we choose to leave the routine chores undone,
Though it's hard to do the petty tasks, where honors there are none,
So I'll resume the old, old role, to comfort while I may
These men of mine who shield me from the struggles of their day.

That they not sink to drudgery, though their bodies droop and tire
That their minds not be dulled by work, but to higher things aspire.
I'll set myself on constant guard, I'll kneel me in the dust;
This world needs strong courageous men, with wisdom which is just.

Summer time, vacation days, but times are busy here; Our clothes
are soiled, our hands are rough, our hearts are full of cheer.
Husband and sons are at the mine, and I am at the shack.
We hope for health, a little wealth, when school days call us back.

\*   \*   \*   \*

As summer approached Dick and Marlin arrived. Wayne and
Jack, high school boys on summer vacation, also showed up. We
now had a full crew. Super was top man and hoist engineer.
Marlin was truck driver and master mechanic. Dave, Dick and I
were underground miners. Wayne and Jack were roustabout
helpers wherever needed. We now had a full complement of
manpower and boypower.

"It's about time we did some more thinking," Super
announced one night during our after-shift bull session. "How do
we get more production without killing ourselves?"

"The rattle-trap Jackhammers Cy cobbled up have served us
okay so far, but sometimes they're a pain in the ass," Dave said.
"We ought to buy a new hammer."

182

Marlin's comment was quick and to the point. "I'm working a double-header every day of the week as it is. The old Kissel is another pain in the ass. If we're gonna increase production I've got to have a truck that'll handle the load."

Flush with optimism and secure with finances, Super agreed. "Pick out the things you want and let's get them."

We bought a Jackhammer, a Dodge dump truck, and a supply of featherweight D-handle shovels to make Dick happy. With good equipment and a full crew we really started to hum. Soon we were shipping two carloads every three days, and receiving between $1500 and $2000 per week to cover our direct expenses and provide, ah, sweet profit. We worked, worked, worked seven days a week, from dawn till done, to sweeten up that profit.

"We've been shipping too much ore as high-grade lately," Super said one evening, as he studied recent settlement sheets. "These big fat checks look good, but we're paying too much royalty and smelter charge when we ship out twelve- or fourteen-dollar rock. The big boys have got our contract rigged so they get most of the velvet when we ship rock that nets out at more than ten dollars a ton. Let's study this thing and see if we can out-smart them."

"We've always figured that eight-dollar rock was our break-even point," Dave said. "But with a full crew and things humming along pretty well, I think we could make money at seven dollars. Some of the old workings are back-filled with seven- or eight-dollar rock. When fill has already been mined and we don't have to blast it, we ought to make her pay."

"That's part of the answer," Super said. "The old-timers back-filled their low-grade to keep from hoisting it to the surface with their horse whim and bucket. They left us a good thing if we're smart enough to see it.

"The best way to make her pay is to sweeten up the low-grade fill with our high-grade ore, and ship it out as ten-dollar rock. That's the point on a sliding scale where we pay the least royalty and smelter charge, and receive the best return on our ore. We'll have to take more samples so we can control the blend we ship, but it'll be worth it.

"There's a limit to our high-grade. At the clip we're shipping we're going to be running out of it pretty quick. We'd better not get too greedy for a fast buck. We'll do a lot better in the long run if we stretch it out."

As consequence of blending our limited high-grade ore with available fill, the life of our mining venture was extended, and our respect for Super's thinking was enhanced.

Camp life soon evolved into a routine. Super realized that the breakfast chef had the nastiest job in camp, so he laid claim to it. Normally Dave was a tranquil and considerate soul. Before breakfast, however, he was insufferably grouchy. Fill him up in a hurry was the way to go, and Super knew that as breakfast chef he could do it.

Super got up early, made a fire, and had the makings of breakfast ready before rousing the crew. He cooked bacon and eggs, and had the pancake batter fortified with canned milk and eggs before calling Dave, who had no time to develop his morning grouch. As Dave devoured his breakfast, Super served the rest of us, each to his liking. Marlin preferred his pancakes fat and his bacon crisp. Dick liked his pancakes thin as crepes and lots of them. I didn't care about most things on the menu as long as my eggs were fried hard.

Super knew that to sustain us throughout a long day's work a hearty breakfast was essential. The rest of us felt that, where Super cooked breakfast, all other camp life drudgery was our responsibility. We minimized it by reducing the dishwashing chore to once a day, and the major housecleaning chores to once a week.

We made a practice after meals of wiping our plates clean with bread and then newspaper or pages from the Sears Roebuck catalog. After brushing crumbs off the table for the benefit of our cat, we placed our plates upside down over the tableware, handy for the next meal. We washed the dishes only after our dinner meal. On Sundays, with Dave the meticulous one serving as boss, we pitched in, cleaned the camp room by room, and boiled up the dirty clothes.

Super seemed always to be thinking. His thinking was not always in a serious vein. I climbed the ladder out of the shaft early one day to prepare lunch. As I automatically unscrewed the bowl of my carbide lamp to remove the sludge, Super pointed toward the air receiver on the mine dump. "Look! Cy, what's that?"

It was a rat, apparently hesitating for a moment before crawling farther. I took careful aim with the bowl of my lamp and pitched a beautiful strike. It hit the air receiver just in front of the rat and ricocheted to land full in his face. In case I had just stunned old mister rat I ran over and stomped him for good.

Super laughed uproariously. He laughed all through lunch and dinner, then chuckled part way through the night. The next morning I had occasion to go near the 50-gallon barrel that contained cooling water for the gasoline engine. There on the ground was a rat's tail.

Oh, oh, now the big laugh made sense. Super had found a drowned rat in the water barrel. When he had tried to remove it by the tail, it had come off. So he had removed the rat bodily and planted it on the air receiver to see what would happen.

The happening exceeded his wildest expectation. He had set a trap. I had taken the bait and killed an already dead rat, not once but twice. When I confronted him with that rat tail between my thumb and forefinger he knew that his private prank was now public. With no further need to restrain his chuckles, he laughed uproariously, and as the butt of his joke I sheepishly joined in. (See illustration on following page.)

Occasionally one of us took a day off to visit mother in Salt Lake City, or friends in Eureka. One Sunday I went to a baseball game. The Eureka team was playing Spanish Fork for the championship. Eureka won the game and staged a celebration. Several members of the team were friends of mine. I must have toasted too many of them too many times before driving back to camp.

**Pitching a beautiful strike was only one phase on the death of a rat**

The road to the mine was hazardous at best. For a tipsy driver it was treacherous. At one point the main road followed a straight and level course to several mines. The road to the Little Spy branched off with a quick turn to the right, then left on a steep upgrade. I took the right turn properly, but turned left too quickly. The car rolled over smack in the middle of the lower road, then continued another roll.

I had removed the cloth top from our Model-A roadster. For some reason I was not been thrown out of the car as it continued to roll. Although the sidehill was steep, the car didn't roll to the bottom.

I was upside down on the floorboard in front of the seat, constrained by the steering column, the emergency brake, and the gear shift lever. Fearful that any brash movement might dislodge the car and start it rolling again, I relaxed to await daylight and get my bearings.

At dawn I could see that the roadster was firmly lodged against a substantial juniper tree. Had I known that, I could have extricated myself at any time. I wiggled free, walked to the mine, and sheepishly confessed my plight to the crew. Marlin said, "I'll put a load on the truck and get some gear together. Then we'll go down and haul her out."

When we arrived at the accident site, he took charge. "Cy," he said, "chain this pulley to a tree up on the hill. Dave can hitch one end of the cable to the truck, and we'll thread it through the pulley. I'll run the other end around the Ford so when we pull it'll turn right side up."

With the truck in compound gear, he inched it forward and the Ford landed on its wheels on the lower road. He checked the gas, water, and crankcase oil, started it, and said, "Okay, take her away and I'll haul this load down to the tipple."

Our Model-A roadster was not seriously damaged in the accident. That pleased me. The indignity of having the escapade was enough to bear. To have ruined our put-put would have been too much.

**Photographs – Little Spy Mine, 1934**

**Upper view – Marlin, pet dog, loaded dump truck**

**Lower view – Truck, ore bin, trestle over waste dump**

    **Opposite page:**

**Top left – Marlin running the hoist**

**Top right – Dave manning the jackhammer**

**Lower – Underground crew: Cy, Dick, and Dave**

# Chapter 16

## Wages Well Spent

As a result of blending our limited high-grade ore with available low-grade fill, the life of our mining venture was extended. However, in the autumn of 1934 the dread day arrived when we ran out of ore and had to abandon the Little Spy mine. Super called a "board of directors" meeting.

As "chairman of the board" and keeper of the purse, Super announced, "Boys, it's been a long struggle, but we finally made it. We've got a hundred thousand dollars stashed away, and that's a lot of money. We can divide it according to the contribution each has made, or we can leave it in the pot and draw on it as our needs arise. Your mother and I have always wanted you to go to college. Here's your chance. Where do you want to go from here?"

After watching the account grow, month after grueling month, and living in anticipation of this happy day, we had no need to ponder. Every working day we had planned for a better life, the dream that had kept us going.

We had left Silver City to its fate as a ghost camp, and returned to Eureka, the queen city of the Tintic Mining District. We had fared well. The district as a whole had not. Most families had abandoned their homes in search of a brighter future. Those who remained were destitute. Among them were miners who had struck it rich leasing, and spent their fortunes as quickly as they made them. Super expressed it succinctly: "They made a bundle and couldn't handle it. Now they don't have a pot to piss in, or a window to throw it out of."

We resolved not to follow that "easy come – easy go" pattern. We had worked long and hard, and sacrificed the pleasures of youth to reach this happy state. "Let's have some fun," we decided, "then get something that can never be squandered: an education."

First we bought a roomy bungalow in Salt Lake City that was easy for Mother to care for and Super to do his thinking in. Then we drew two thousand dollars apiece, and four of us enrolled at the University of Utah beginning the winter quarter of 1935. Dave majored in Philosophy, Marlin in Speech, Dick and I in Engineering. We developed a routine: Study until eleven o'clock in the rec-room, shoot the bull over a glass of Dave's home brew (he was a good brewmaster) until midnight, then get to bed.

My $2,000 didn't last long. A college man ought to have a car. I purchased a brand new De Soto four-door sedan, a slick automobile, black, with white side wall tires. She cost me $995 cash. With a car like that a man ought to have some clothes, so I drove down to Arthur Frank's, the fanciest clothier in town. When I walked in, not a customer was in sight. Three salesmen were discussing something. It must have been an interesting subject because they ignored me for several minutes. Perhaps that should have been expected because in my working garb I was an unlikely customer. Eventually one of them deigned to approach me, "May I help you?"

"I'd like a coupla pair of slacks, one tan and one gray. Maybe I'd better have a pair of brown ones, too."

"What?" was his incredulous response. He measured my waist, and observed that in my heavy work shoes he couldn't get a good inseam measurement.

"That's all right. I need some shoes anyway. Give me a pair of black Florsheims, and I guess I'd better have a pair of brown ones, too."

"Will this be cash or charge?"

"Cash."

"Hmmm. Will there be anything else?"

"Yes, I'd like a suit and an overcoat. Top of the line Hart, Shaffner & Marx. And I'll need a couple of sport jackets, half a dozen Arrow shirts, and a few accessories. I'd better get a tuxedo, too, and the paraphernalia that goes with it – patent leather shoes and stuff like that."

By that time the salesman's associates had scented a good thing. They wanted to give service, and I assume to share in the commission. They hovered over me as though I were Mr. Rockefeller himself. I paid the bill, and with the help of two deferential salesmen, carried the loot to my new automobile. I was clearly the best customer they had seen in many days.

As a college man, decked out in proper attire and owner of a fancy automobile, I wanted one more thing, the most important of all, a nice girl friend to take dancing on Saturday nights. I'd had scant opportunity for social life since leaving high school. I figured out a likely strategy to get back in circulation, then plied it with consummate skill.

Taking matters in the order of priority, I started with the first essential: finding the right girl. All students on campus had occasion to visit the Administration Building, and some of the girls used the entrance as a parade ground. Whenever I had free time, I loitered at a vantage point and observed the promenade. After several stints of surveillance, I zeroed in on a fascinating specimen of femininity. Smitten by an ardor that transcends thought, I hastened to approach my quarry before losing confidence.

"Excuse me, miss," I began. "I'm new here and would like to get the feel of campus life. There's a get-acquainted tag dance Wednesday afternoon at the Union Building. I don't like to go places by myself. I'm kind of shy and bashful. However, I know a gorgeous creature when I see one, and am bold enough to ask if you might go with me?"

"I'm new here, too," she said, and looked me in the eye,

The mystery of her momentary silence bore heavily upon me. She continued, "I think I'd like that. Let's plan on it."

As advertised, this get-acquainted dance was a mixer, a tag dance. No sooner had I escorted my prize onto the floor than I was tapped on the shoulder. Eventually I got her back, but then I was tapped again. To every stag man all the girls on the floor were fair game, and mine was the fairest. I began to wonder. Is this what I want? She had confided her aspiration to be a thespian, whatever that was. Did I want a thespian to share with the world, or an ordinary girl to share the aspirations of an ordinary guy? As my mother had said, "today's peacock is tomorrow's feather duster."

While mulling the problem, I glanced at the girls' line and was immediately struck by a willowy brunette who had a special lilt in her look. It was not a come hither lilt, just a clear and calm expression of lightness and buoyancy that urged me forward. "May we dance?"

This girl, Margaret Stratton, had rhythm from her toes to the top of her pretty head. Half way around the dance floor I knew I'd found the answer to my dreams. "I'm tied up this afternoon, but I'd love to take you to the Rainbow Rendezvous Saturday night. Harry James and his orchestra will be there. Can you make it?"

"Yes, I can make it."

What a life! I had nice clothes, a spiffy automobile, and a lovely girl to take dancing every Saturday night. However, over time a problem developed. I hadn't taken into account the depth of my attachment for this girl. Saturday nights came around too infrequently. How do I reconcile my lifelong desire for knowledge with my newly acquired longing of the heart? Oh well, I rationalized, the Saturday night limitation was arbitrary. I'd have to bend it a little. Not abandon it, but merely adapt to change in circumstance. Having succumbed to that bit of wisdom, I found it easy to yield to the yearnings of my heart. In doing so, I found that life was doubly sweet. Without sacrificing my love of learning, I gained not just a girl friend, but a companion for life.

Our family bull sessions were rewarding. Mother basked quietly as she saw the seeds she had nourished grown to maturity. The four college brothers shared interests of the day, reminisced on hardships of the past, relished the pleasures of the present, and planned for the future.

Planning for the future was Super's prime preoccupation. He devoted his time to scouting the mining districts of the state, listening to old-timers describe "where a man might strike it rich," and investigating the most promising of those stories. When he found something of interest he joined in our student bull session.

Super's proposals usually drew skeptical reaction. We knew that his perpetual optimism sometimes merged into gullibility. However, if they survived our critical review, we joined him for a weekend investigation. Occasionally he found a worthwhile project and we joined in the enterprise. These activities provided summer employment and sufficient income to maintain the family reserve. No jobs were available. We manufactured our own.

No jobs were available unless one had special qualifications. As an engineering student, I was able to find specialty work, and thereby maintain my classy standard of living without having to tap the family finances. One of my fellow students told me of a job possibility.

Secretary of Agriculture Henry A. Wallace had developed a program to map the entire country as a basis for studies of land utilization.

He contracted the taking of aerial photographs to commercial firms, and established three photogrammetry offices within his Department to convert the aerial photographs to corrected scale maps. One of those offices was in Salt Lake City. I talked to the manager about job prospects.

He described the work, then leveled with me. "Somewhere down the line this project will taper off," he said. "When it does, at least one of the three offices will be closed. I don't want to get the axe, so I run the most efficient operation possible. I hire engineering students. You young guys have good eyes and know how to handle a slide rule. For your convenience, I've set a work schedule from four o'clock to midnight. We don't tolerate chit chat. We pay four dollars a day, and work a five day week. If you're interested, fill out an application."

I filled out an application and started work the following Monday. It was a good job, and I stayed with it until a better one came along.

Twenty dollars a week was handsome pay, but working forty hours a week cut into my study time. An opportunity arose where I could make about the same money without spending much time. This was also a government sponsored activity. It seemed the only work available was government sponsored.

The departments of Civil and Mining Engineering at the University of Utah desired an underground mine for the teaching of advanced surveying. The Works Progress Administration and the National Youth Administration approached the university, seeking sponsors for projects that provide work for the unemployed. If the university would sponsor and provide supervision for such a project, the government agencies would provide the manpower. The concept of a Model Mine, long dormant, became a reality.

The WPA provided unemployed miners as foremen, the NYA provided youths as apprentice miners, and the university provided me as supervision. At a salary of $75 per month I was in clover. I merely had to oversee the work, keep the records, and prepare the payroll. It was a good job while it lasted, and it lasted two years.

When the Model Mine project was finished, Professor Lewis, head of the Mining Engineering department, said to me, "Walt Landwehr is going to be needing a draftsman part-time to transcribe his field notes onto permanent maps. I told him of your background. He said to send you in to see him. You might be able to tag along on some of his field investigations. This might be a good chance to learn a few things that aren't covered in class."

Dr. Walt Landwehr, a highly respected geologist, was head of the Western Exploration Division of the American Smelting & Refining Company. I relished the opportunity to fly under his wing. We talked things over.

"The girl who does my drafting will be leaving pretty soon to have a baby," he told me. "Whenever you have free time, come down to the office and she'll help you get started. When you get the hang of things and you're on your own, I'll leave my notes on the drafting table. You can come in at your convenience and transcribe them. This is temporary until she's able to return. At that time we'll see what happens.

That was more than I could have hoped for. This was not textbook stuff. This was the real world of mining, geology, and exploration. Like a sponge seeking moisture, I absorbed the drafting routine quickly. From time to time Dr. Landwehr scheduled his field investigations so I could accompany him. On these trips he was my mentor on ethical as well as technical matters and we became good friends. As his confidant, I learned some of the ways of the wicked world.

Upon investigating one mining property, Dr. Landwehr quickly rejected as worthless the appearance of mineralization exposed in the underground workings.

"Walt," I asked, "if the prospects of finding ore are so remote, why does the company fare so well on the Salt Lake Stock Exchange?"

"The local Exchange lists a lot of penny stocks sponsored by mine promoters. If promoters can't sell stock based on mineral prospects, they sell it based on their surface plant. Do you see that nice building? It houses a Diesel engine, a compressor, and a generator. It's nothing but a carrot that the promoter uses to entice his clientele to invest in the company. The average investor will say to himself, 'If the company is so sure of its future that it will spend this kind of money, it must be a good thing. I'll buy some of the stock.' The average investor doesn't realize that on mine promotions more money is squandered on surface plant than is spent on underground exploration."

"Walt," I asked further, "why does the penny stock market fluctuate so wildly?"

"On the Denver and the Salt Lake Exchanges, the stocks that fluctuate wildly are of mining companies that have only prospects. They're not producing companies, so the market value depends on hope. The promoters don't have the resources to bring a mine into production.

When sale of their stock based on their surface plant tapers off, their next big hope is to interest a strong company in their property. If the word gets out that A.S.& R., for example, is

197

interested in a company, their stock goes up. If we send out a field party and the word gets out, the stock jumps again. If we take an option on the property and start serious exploration, the stock skyrockets. If at any time we pull out, the stock plummets.

"You can see that if the promoter is privy to our plans, he can buy cheap, sell dear, and make a killing. So can the engineers and executives in the firm making the exploration. I'm sorry to say some fellows get greedy and take advantage of their inside information. The losers are the investors who don't know what they're doing."

This information alerted me to some of the wiles of mine promoters. I was not prepared, however, to divine the devious machinations of one master practitioner of the craft.

**Bargains abound in the Penny Stock Market**

\* \* \* \*

A. D. Wallon, the president of a small company, offered me a summer job at his mine near Rio Tinto, Nevada. He needed an

198

engineer to survey his property and prepare geologic maps of the surface and underground workings. This engineer would also supervise the mining activities of the crew. Although the crew consisted of only two men, and the salary of four dollars a day was no great enticement, I accepted the job. The title "Mine Superintendent" of the Grimes Homestake Consolidated Mining Corporation tickled my vanity. It would also appear impressive on my resume sometime in the future. A young fellow has to look ahead.

My first priority, after my boss showed me around the property and returned to his office, was to concentrate on underground operations. An adit had been driven along the course of a narrow vein for several hundred feet. The vein was exposed in the roof (commonly called the back) of the adit. The vein had split into segments at various places, and drifts had been run along each segment. The underground workings thus resembled a felled tree with a trunk and several branches.

At the end of each drift the vein was at maximum width compared with the usual exposure. The crew was driving ahead on the main trunk where the vein showed scant promise of developing a worthwhile ore deposit. I therefore moved the crew to the most likely branch. As we drove forward on that branch the vein narrowed. I moved the crew to the next most likely branch, then to the next and the next until no good showings remained. That was the situation when Mr. Wallon arrived to show three prospective investors, with their own eyes, the many possibilities of wealth that this mine displayed.

Alas, there were no possibilities to display!

"Holy ke-rist, Cy!" my boss exploded when he cornered me in private. "Don't you know nothing! Maybe it's partly my fault for not leveling with you, but now you know what it's all about. Next time I drive clients out here I want to see a nice vein structure at the face of every one of those drifts."

Knowing what it's all about, I followed Mr. Wallon's instructions. When the school term approached, I gave him the maps I had prepared and asked for my pay. "Let's see now," he said. "Beyond what you've already drawn, I've got you down for sixty days at four dollars a day. That's $240. I can give you a check, or if you want some of it in stock, you can have it at two cents a share." Knowing what it's all about, I took my summer wages in cash.

An exploratory shaft being driven nearby then struck high grade copper ore. When this became public knowledge, the stock of Grimes Homestake jumped to eighteen cents. If I had taken stock for my work, and sold it at the right time, I would have $2160 for my summer wages. Such were the vicissitudes of the penny stock market.

# Chapter 17

# Banner Mining Venture – The Last Hurrah

Dick, the youngest of the four brothers who had enrolled together at the University of Utah, left college in favor of an early marriage. Dave, Marlin, and I graduated in June 1939, and my college sweetheart received her teaching certificate. We were married the day following our graduation exercises.

The depression, although still rampant throughout the country, was viewed by our family as merely a bad chapter in the ups and downs of the past. Hope surged ceaselessly in Super's veins. One evening, after spending a week prowling around Idaho, he shared his latest burst of enthusiasm.

"Fellows," he said, "I've chanced upon a mining venture that's too good to be true. It's the old Banner mine, about thirty miles northeast of Idaho City. It's too small to be of interest to a big company, and too big for a small operator to handle. This is just the thing for us. We've got the manpower and plenty of equipment from previous jobs. This weekend let's go take a look."

We took a look, and found the Banner Mine ripe for plucking. The history of this mine was the stuff of both fact and romantic legend. The fact was that it had shipped more than three million dollars in silver to the U.S. Mint. The legend was woven into stories of the early days, ox teams, fabulously rich ore, hardships, and successes.

Adventurers heading west to the California gold fields stumbled upon a vast accumulation of gold-bearing gravels in central Idaho. Thousands of men, and a few harlots, poured into Idaho City, the site of those gravels, to reap the rewards of this placer bonanza. Prospectors soon roamed the surrounding hills in search of the mother lode, the source of that gravel. None found it. However, in 1864 James H. Hawley, later Governor of Idaho, discovered an outcropping of rich silver ore. He called his property the Banner mine.

Hawley sold his claims to a storekeeper who developed the property. He installed a 20-stamp mill to crush the ore, and amalgamation plates to separate the silver from the waste material. He then sold out to the Elmira Silver Mining Company of Elmira, New York. Elmira operated the mine and made a handsome profit year after year.

Mr. Vivian A. Thorne, later the Mayor and a longtime resident of Idaho City, was the next owner. He described the circumstance of his purchase, and the subsequent history of the property.

"I came to this country in 1889 as representative of an English company. I was authorized to offer the Elmira Company $700,000 for the Banner mine. Well, I offered Elmira $600,000 for the mine, and offered the resident manager $100,000 to help swing the deal. The manager rejected my overture, and Elmira held out for a million. I bided my time.

"While awaiting developments, I fell in love with this part of the world. I severed relationship with my English company and took a job as accountant for Elmira. As such, I knew all the financial aspects of the mine. When the price of silver dropped to 42 cents an ounce, the Elmira company got disheartened. By 1893 I was able to buy the property in my own name.

"I didn't have the resources to operate the mine myself, so ever since I've been trying to interest a big company to come in with me. With the help of my son Rupert, I've kept the mine workings open, but now I'm getting old and can't hold on much longer. I'm ready to deal." We negotiated a Bond & Lease agreement, a contract peculiar to the mining industry. The purchase price is retired through royalty payments on the ore shipped. As owners of this fabled mine, we went to work.

In the early days a vertical shaft had been sunk on the sidehill where the veins had been exposed. As mining continued to greater depth, pumping out the water that seeped from the surface became prohibitively expensive. An adit was therefore driven to drain the mine and intercept the veins at the 485-foot level of the shaft. This 3,600-foot adit was driven in the late 1880s. The ore mined between the adit level and the lower reaches served by the shaft paid for driving the adit. Then the silver panic struck. Soon thereafter, Mr. Thorne acquired the property.

As new operators of this mine, we figured we could net $100,000 for every hundred feet we stripped the ore below the adit level. A large amount of preliminary work was required. We approached it with gusto.

We moved our accumulation of mining equipment to the portal of the adit, then planned some more. "Let's get a diesel engine to drive our air compressor," Marlin suggested. "I know where we can buy a good one cheap. I've studied diesels in the Navy, so if we have trouble I'm sure we can fix 'em." We bought a diesel.

"It's a long way to the assay office," I said. "We ought to be independent and set up our own facilities. At school I got an A in assaying, so I guess we can rely on my results." We bought a muffle furnace, some scales, and a supply of crucibles, cupels, litharge, and soda ash that would be required for gold and silver assays.

"We've got to run an air line from the compressor to our working face," Super said. "It has to be at least four inches in diameter, or we'll lose too much pressure. That'll cost a pretty penny."

"I don't think so," Marlin responded. "We'll cut the tubes out of some of those old steam boilers with an acetylene torch, and weld them end to end along the adit." We bought an acetylene generator and a supply of calcium carbide, oxygen, and welding rod. Marlin laid a compressed-air line, leak-proof all the way.

As his part in the preliminary work, Super built a substantial shop and compressor annex. Dave, Dick, and I cleaned out the adit and blasted a station. From the station, we sank a winze, an underground shaft, for mining out the ore below the adit level.

**Upper view – Surface plant**

**Center view – Living quarters**

**Lower view – Cemetery, occupied since 1865**

**Photographs at Banner Mine, 1940**

Camp life blossomed during the summer and autumn seasons. Wayne, Dick, and I were married. The working crew of Father and six sons was joined by Mother, the three brides, and one baby who had made an appearance. There was no more camp cooking by the boys. There were nice long strolls in the woods for the girls, huckleberrying on Sundays, table tennis and target practice evenings. It was a happy time in an idyllic setting, the culmination to a dream for which we had long striven.

An isolated snow-bound camp was no place for women or children, however, and on the approach of winter they returned home. The working crew missed their companionship and their many contributions to camp life. Most of all, they, and especially I, missed Marge, whose very presence kept our spirits high, as did her delicious cooking. She baked three loaves of bread every day and cooked the venison so it tasted like baby beef.

Our dead work dragged out longer than foreseen. In late autumn of 1941 we made plans to continue working throughout the winter. We felled trees for Super to fashion into mine timbers, laid in supplies of diesel fuel, blasting powder, and lots of food. We sank the winze to a depth of 100 feet as planned, and were preparing to drive drifts along the vein, then mine the ore blocked out.

Our gamble in developing the Banner mine to the production stage was about to pay off. The work was in capable hands, I reasoned. and my presence full-time not essential for success of the venture, Besides, I missed Marge. So I opted to fulfill another dream: to obtain a Masters Degree in Mining Engineering. With the financial help of scholarships and grants, I returned to the University of Utah and spent only my spare time at the mine. I was there when catastrophe struck.

We had harnessed a small stream near our bunkhouse to serve as a miniature power plant. Descending water from the stream drove our make-shift waterwheel, which in turn drove an automobile generator wired to a storage battery. This provided lights for the camp and power for a radio. One evening the radio was alive with news: Pearl Harbor had been bombed. The

Japanese had performed "that dastardly act." The date was December 7, 1941. We were at war!

"It looks like we'll have to abandon our winter plans," Dave said, "and see what Uncle Sam wants to do with us."

"We've got to get out of here in a hurry," Super said. "It's snowing pretty hard right now. If we wait till morning we'll never get over the summit and we'll be stuck here till spring breaks."

"Let's figure this thing out," Marlin suggested. "If we high-tail for home we'll lose everything we've put into this venture. If we wait till spring, we'll just lose that much more. You can be damn sure of one thing. We'll have to pull out one time or another. They're not going to let a bunch of young guys mine silver when there is a war going on. The sooner we take our medicine, the quicker we'll recover."

"I'm afraid," Super said, "we'll never recover. You boys will get wrapped up in the war effort. You'll get spread out in all directions and never get back to finish the job. I feel it in my bones, goddamn it."

Super's shoulders slumped perceptibly. Sensing his deep emotion, we quietly loaded our most precious valuables in our vehicles and headed for home. On the way, Dave and I had ample time to assess the present, reflect on the past, and contemplate the future. His college studies in philosophy had given him insight into concepts foreign to me. My practical bent provided a balancing viewpoint. Our close association throughout successes and failures had led us to similar views on many of the important things of life.

"We're in a different ball game, Dave. Shall we pass, punt, or take a time-out?"

"It's different all right, Cy. In our younger days we had a fun life. It was a rough life too, and maybe that was for the best. It taught us to face both the hardships of hobo life and the realities of the depression. Now we face the unknown. I guess we'd better call a time-out to catch our bearings."

"Ever since we got into Lend-Lease the country has been working out of the depression," I said. "With war upon us,

206

things will really boom. There will be opportunities for some, but not for us. The sad fact is, we did well as family entrepreneurs during the depression, but that's over and now we'll be on our own.

"We've had our ups and our downs. At the Little Spy, we won against odds that we faced from the start. At the Banner, we licked the problems we could foresee, but lost against odds beyond our control. If we can get back together after the war, we'll know what the odds are and recoup our losses. That's a dream to keep us going while we're doing what Uncle Sam tells us. Let's enjoy our time-out while we can."

# Chapter 18

# Dispersion of the Entrepreneurial Clan

Our old world was no more. Our days as rogues, hoboes, and entrepreneurs were all in the past. We knew we were bidding those happy, sad, exhilarating days a permanent farewell. In one brief moment we had lost it all. All, that is, except the entrepreneurial spirit that accepts misfortune in stride and carries alive the torch of hope. Super's shoulders slumped but in the spirit of hope his indomitable will prevailed. He would persevere; his sons could do no less. Our entrepreneurial team was disbanded but as individuals we would carry on.

While awaiting "Greetings" from the armed services, we thought of how we could best contribute to the war effort. The U.O.P., short for Utah Ordnance Plant, a large facility in Salt Lake City for manufacturing .30 and .50 caliber ammunition, provided the best opportunity.

Dave applied for work at the UOP and was hired as a foreman in the inspection department. Maintaining decorum among the hundreds of female workers doing repetitive work was a challenge. As a single male among many females looking for fun, a husband, or both, he married one of them, which removed him as a distracting target.

Over time he became discontented with his contribution to the war effort and decided to apply for officer training in the Navy. During his physical exam the doctor said, "I'm afraid you're a little too short to be an officer. We all shrink a bit during the day, then recover at night. I'll tell you what to do. You have a good sleep tonight and I'll see you first thing in the morning. I think you will then be tall enough to be an officer."

"The hell with it!" Dave exploded. "If I'm not man enough to be an officer in the afternoon, I'm not man enough in the morning. I'll join the Navy and be a seaman, gob, or whatever they call misfits." He stomped out, joined the Navy, and after basic training, volunteered for a construction battalion, the Sea Bees.

He served in the Sea Bees throughout the war. As a frequent volunteer for duty in demolition squadrons, small units formed to cripple or demolish enemy targets with explosives, he was moved from post to post in New Guinea, Guam, Borneo, New Hebrides, and New Caledonia.

The officer charged with censoring mail called Dave in. "You're a smart guy," he said. "I'll have you censor the mail. Strike out the sensitive stuff. If you have a questionable letter, give it to me. This is between us. The men will never know you're hip to their affairs."

Dave's service as censor gave him insight into the thoughts, dreams, and frustrations of his buddies, and the boredom they felt. He decided to improve the morale and reduce the boredom by typing news of interest in a pamphlet and circulating it within the group. His superior approved, and offered clerical help and paper for the project. Dave prepared the first issue, invited others to contribute, and was soon editing a weekly flier that was eagerly read by officers and enlisted men alike. The last issue proclaimed in bold type, "The War is Over." That marked the end of Dave's venture in bringing fresh hope to bored Sea Bees in the far islands of the Pacific.

After the war Dave took advantage of the G.I. Bill and enrolled at the University of California, Los Angeles. Upon completing courses in personnel management he applied for work at the City of Los Angeles. Hired as a civil service examiner, he worked his way up the ladder and retired as principal personnel analyst. He devoted his retirement years planting and nurturing roses, and at age 88 died of pneumonia, complicated by lungs weakened through years of breathing silica dust as a hard-rock miner.

Marlin was hired by the Utah Ordnance Plant as general foreman in the mechanical department, to supervise either mechanics or machinists as the needs arose. He was barely organized when he was asked to take an unspecified position at a hush-hush facility in Washington State, known only as Pasco. He accepted. The position was Superintendent of Transportation. The facility was called the Hanford Engineering Works during the secretive days, later as the Hanford Atomic Energy Plant.

Hanford was behind schedule recruiting the many skilled craftsmen required to man the plant. Management knew, from personnel records, of Marlin's speech background and his knowledge of things practical. His superior told him, "Take a break from your transportation job and serve as our national recruiter. Recruit mechanics, machinists, carpenters, electricians, tinsmiths, and others skilled in the trades. Do it your way, Just do it."

Marlin's way to "just do it" was to travel the country, advertise for craftsmen in the next city he would visit, interview applicants, and hire the ones deemed fit for Hanford. He was perpetually traveling and never had time to be home. His wife Dorothy flew to Oklahoma City to be with him briefly. While there she contracted a virulent form of polio and died in his arms within twenty-four hours. Her sister Jean looked after his little boy, and later married Marlin.

The inability of medical science to cure the disease that struck Dorothy weighed heavily on Marlin. As an undergraduate, he had taken a course in gross anatomy. It was a memory course used to weed out pre-medical students unlikely to survive the rigors of medical study. For Marlin, it was a snap course. Why not pursue a medical career, he wondered. After the war, he returned to Salt Lake City, enrolled in the newly formed School of Medicine at the University of Utah, and graduated with honors.

With his medical degree in hand, he served Internship and Residency at the Naval Hospital in San Francisco, then established a general practice in Cloverdale, California. To perform surgery he used the nearest hospital, which was in Santa Rosa. To reduce travel time he bought a plane.

One Sunday he flew to Chico, California to do a little bird hunting with friends. One of them later told us the sad news: "He took off, circled a couple of times, wagged his wings, and headed for home. The plane suddenly tipped down, then dived to the ground." He had suffered a heart attack and died at age 48.

In June 1942 I was awarded an MS degree in mining engineering and elected into membership in The Society Of The Sigma Xi, the national honorary research fraternity. The day I took my comprehensive examination for the advanced degree my thoughts were in turmoil. Marge was expecting, and that day gave birth to the first of our five daughters.

Sensing the need of steady income, I took a job as supervisor, ballistics department, of the Utah Ordnance Plant, which was managed by the Remington Arms Company. After observing my performance for a few months, that company transferred me to its headquarters in Bridgeport, Connecticut. As research metallurgist in the technical department, I worked on classified projects sponsored by the Army Ordnance Department.

After the war my entrepreneurial spirit prevailed, and I chose to be a big fish in a little pool. I took a job as manager of a small pulp and paper mill in Maine that was near bankruptcy. I put on my manager's hat by day and my machine-designer's hat by night. The company prospered, then was bought by Lily Tulip Cup Corporation. It prospered further, but I was back in a big pool of corporate environment not to my liking. I resigned and followed other interests.

For a few years I served as executive director of the Maine Good Roads Association and editor of its monthly magazine The *Maine Trail*. When that grew stale I put on my chemist's hat and developed an insect repellent called Repel. I designed and built a machine to perform all the functions of bottling and packing the product, and formed a company to merchandise it. However, for me the fun was in developing something rather than selling it, so I sold the business and moved to a retirement community, Sun City West, Arizona, where I keep busy at my computer.

Dick, fourth of the six sons, served as a mechanic at the Utah Ordnance Plant, then transferred to Hanford where he worked on atomic stuff until his retirement in Washington State. He died at 82 from a combination of breathing silica dust as a hard-rock miner during his younger years and ignoring his health during his later years.

Wayne, fifth of the boys, volunteered for the Navy but at the induction center was summarily assigned to the Army. As "the orneriest soldier in the Army," (his words) he joined the paratroops and served in the 82nd Airborne Division. Except for a bad back suffered by dropping from low height behind enemy lines in Germany and Occupied France, he survived unscathed. After the war he tried chicken farming and trucking, then the trades – welding, carpentry, and machining – prior to retiring as a do-anything gentleman farmer in Talent, Oregon.

Jack, sixth of the boys, was not accepted by the armed services because of an enlarged "athlete's heart" from playing too much tournament tennis. He worked at an airplane assembly plant in San Diego, and after the war built a lucrative sales agency which when sold provided for a pleasant retirement in Salt Lake City.

Father/Pappy/Super was to the end an entrepreneur. He decided to build a mill to grind a ledge of limestone into rock dust, an inert material used in spraying coal mines to reduce the explosive hazard of fine particles that settle throughout coal mine workings. It was a big project. Before bringing it to fruition he died at age 77, his body worn out by entrepreneurial struggle. His indomitable will was still intact, as was his optimism. That spirit had an enduring influence on his six sons.

Mother, who supported the clan in all endeavors and provided the glue to hold it together in times of adversity, died in Salt Lake City at age 94. Her legacy was instilling in her sons not only the love of learning but always the determination to strive for the higher things of life.

Marge, entrepreneur by osmosis and integral member of the clan, spends her boundless energy mothering our five daughters far from the nest, and keeps me free of distraction during this writing venture. She provides the care that makes for all of us happy and wholesome lives.

Rogues, Hoboes, and Entrepreneurs; Coping with the Great Depression has reached the end. The surviving rogues have grown to manhood and dispersed. This hobo relives his youthful exploits in memory only. The entrepreneurs have lost the spirit that sustained the clan until the Banner mine was abandoned. The war ended the Great Depression, and therefore the need to cope with it. All of which marks closure of this book.

# GLOSSARY
## and explanatory notes.

Migratory worker is a generic term which in the hobo vernacular is statified in several categories, each bearing a distinct connotation.

Transient means passing through and stopping briefly. Vagrant -- one who wanders with no fixed home or means of livelihood and ekes out a living by panhandling or stealing. Vagabond -- one who wanders without visible means of support; a disreputable character who roams in an idle, carefree, manner. Hobo -- one who migrates from place to place in search of seasonal work. Tramp -- One who wanders in search of work when beggaring or petty thieving are inadequate for survival. Bum -- one who would rather sponge than work. The term stresses worthlessness with implications of laziness and often drunkenness. All transients wander. While wandering, the vagrant panhandles, the vagabond dreams, the hobo works, the tramp steals, and the bum drinks.

Bindlestiff -- a transient who carries his gear in a bindle or a bag. Bindle is hobo lingo for bundle. A wino is a tramp or a bum who leads the life of an alcoholic. A sundowner is a transient who arrives at a work camp in time for the evening meal but not in time to earn it. A homeguard is a tramp who remains in one area rather than migrate. A mission stiff is a tramp who lives out his life on handouts from a mission.

Railroading terms

Bull -- a railroad detective who patrols against vandalism and hoboes. A yard bull remains in the railroad yard. A riding bull stays with the train to destination. Shifter -- a close-coupled locomotive used in the classification yards of a railroad to "make up" outgoing trains. Each may be made up of various types of railroad cars: Flatcar -- a platform mounted on wheels for hauling lumber, automobiles, machinery. Gondola -- a

215

shallow open-top car for hauling ore, coal, and similar bulk materials. Boxcar -- an enclosed car for hauling grain, paper products, and materials in general that must be protected against the weather. Reefer -- a boxcar refrigerated with ice in a special compartment at the top of the car. Caboose -- the traveling home of the crew. Affectionately called "crummy," it is the last car of a train.

Tipple -- 1. an apparatus for unloading freight cars by tipping or overturning them; 2. an overhead trestle from which bulk materials may be transferred from truck to rail or from one railroad car to another.

Hobo terms

Jungle -- a hobo campsite where water, firewood, cans, and other amenities may be found. A jungle is frequently maintained by local authorities to keep hoboes away from the community. Punk -- bread, usually stale, the mainstay of hobo fare. Boodle town -- a town or city where the sheriff or marshall is in cahoots with the judge. The money they receive for feeding prisoners is greater than their expense. They keep the jail/pokey full by rounding up transients on vagrancy charges. Kangaroo court -- a mock tribunal held by inmates of a jail. Hoover blankets -- nighttime coverings of heavy wrapping paper torn from the inside of a boxcar; named after the president, as was also Hooverville, for a community of hovels.

The manner in which hoboes ride trains is expressed variously as: Riding the deck -- the top of a boxcar. Riding outside -- exposed to the elements. Riding inside -- protected from the weather as in a boxcar.

Riding the rods -- on the undercarriage of a railroad car, a hazardous position. Riding the blinds -- between the locomotive and the baggage car; provides a fast trip on a passenger train, and safe if the engine crew doesn't object.

Mining terms

Ore -- mineralized material that can be mined at a profit. Outcrop -- surface exposure of a vein, or other evidence of a mineral deposit. Float -- fragment of ore that has been transported from an outcrop to a lower elevation by gravity and weathering processes. Gangue -- non-metallic minerals such as quartz, calcite, and barite that are associated with ore minerals. Waste -- country rock or mineralized material too low in value to be classified as ore, but that must be removed during development work

Miner -- in general, an underground worker in a mine. In a hard-roak mine he is the lead man in a crew at one working face. He drills a "round of holes" and does the blasting. The mucker shovels the "muck" broken by the previous shift into minecars. The trammer "trams" or pushes the loaded minecar to the shaft station. The cager provides an empty car and sends the loaded one to the surface in the elevator (cage). A nipper provides blasting materials and drill steel to all the miners on the shift. A timberman installs stulls and posts wherever "heavy ground" is encountered. A boomer is a special breed of miner. He works a job until wanderlust or an alcoholic binge moves him on. He goes from one mining district to another, gaining experience along the way. He enjoys a warm welcome wherever he applies for work.

Dynamite is a powerful explosive. For the trade it is dispersed in an absorbent medium. This product, in cartridge (stick) form, is called blasting gelatin, or simply powder. This powder is tamped by the miner in each of the holes he has drilled. To detonate it he uses a blasting cap, called a primer. To provide time for safe exit from the working face he uses fuse. The central core in the fuse burns at a fixed rate, about one foot per minute. The miner cuts from a coil equal lengths of fuse for each hole. To each length he crimps a primer and laces it into a stick of powder. He tamps this and other sticks into the holes, then cuts off the ends of selected fuse lengths in amount so the charges fire in desired sequence. He then "splits" the open ends of the fuses to expose the central core of incendiary powder, "spits" (ignites) them with the flame of his carbide lamp, shouts fire, and heads with the crew to the shaft station.

Farming terms

In harvesting forage crops such as cultivated alfalfa or wild volunteer grasses, a <u>mower</u> is used to cut the growth to within a few inches of ground level. In this machine a toothed knife is made to oscillate across a similarly toothed fixed knife. The cut crop, spread across the field, is gathered into <u>windrows</u> by means of a <u>rake</u>. If the hay is to be hauled to a barn by <u>hayracks</u> or <u>boats</u>. the windrows are gathered into <u>cocks</u> by <u>spike pitchers</u>. If the hay is to be stacked in the field, <u>bullrakes,</u> also called buckrakes, may be used to move the hay from the windrows to the derrick at the stack, thus making the cocking operation unnecessary.

In harvesting grain, a <u>reaper</u> is used to cut the crop and assemble it into bundles tied with straw string. The bundles are stood upright in the form of shocks. When dried, the bundles are moved to the <u>threshing machine</u> where the grain is separated from the chaff. That was the old way. Modern methods combine the reaping and the threshing in one operation, accomplished by a <u>combined harvester</u>.

<u>And found</u> neans with meals and a place to sleep. <u>Cookee</u> originally meant assistant cook. In western ranches where there was no assistant, the cookee was the cook. <u>Campjack</u> was both the cookee and the maintainer of the camp. In sheephearding parlance: <u>To trail</u> is to move the herd from one area to a distant area. To <u>lamb out</u> is to oversee the birth of the lamb crop in the spring. To <u>dock</u> is to cut off the tails of lambs. To <u>dip</u> is to force lambs through a medicinal solution to kill ticks. To <u>castrate</u> is to remove the testicles from male lambs and make of them <u>wethers</u>.

# ABOUT THE AUTHOR

Cy Greenhalgh was born in 1914 at Silver City, Utah, the third of six sons. When he graduated from high school in 1932, college was only a dream. Then a family mining venture prospered and he attended the University of Utah, where he graduated with a Bachelor's Degree in Mining Engineering in 1939 and a Master's Degree in 1942. He worked for the Bureau of Mines investigating strategic mineral deposits in Montana, Nevada and Utah, and as one in a family of entrepreneurs, developed a silver mine in Idaho. During WW II he served as ballistics supervisor at the Utah Ordinance Plant in Salt Lake City, Utah, then as a research metallurgist at Remington Arms Company in Bridgeport, Connecticut. After the war he was manager of a pulp and paper mill in Old Town, Maine, followed by a stint as executive director of the Maine Good Roads Association and editor of its publication *The Maine Trail*. As a sideline, he developed the insect repellent Repel, formed a company to manufacture it, and, when merchandising became a burden, sold the business and retired. He is the father of five daughters and lives with his wife of sixty years in the retirement community Sun City West, Arizona.

Printed in the United States
3281

9 781588 200860